LEAVE 'EM
WANTING
MORE

children's ministry that thrills as it teaches

sheela
daley

LEAVE 'EM
WANTING
MORE

children's ministry that thrills as it teaches

TATE PUBLISHING & Enterprises

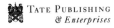

TATE PUBLISHING
& Enterprises

Tate Publishing is committed to excellence in the publishing industry. Our staff of highly trained professionals, including editors, graphic designers, and marketing personnel, work together to produce the very finest books available. The company reflects the philosophy established by the founders, based on Psalms 68:11,

"THE LORD GAVE THE WORD AND GREAT WAS THE COMPANY OF THOSE WHO PUBLISHED IT."

If you would like further information, please contact us:

1.888.361.9473 | www.tatepublishing.com

TATE PUBLISHING & Enterprises, LLC | 127 E. Trade Center Terrace

Mustang, Oklahoma 73064 USA

Leave 'Em Wanting More

This title is also available as a Tate Out Loud product. Visit www.tatepublishing.com for more information.

Scripture quotations marked "NIV" are taken from the *Holy Bible, New International Version* ®, Copyright © 1973, 1978, 1984 by International Bible Society. Used by permission of Zondervan Publishing House. All rights reserved.

Scripture quotations marked "Msg" are taken from *The Message*, Copyright © 1993, 1994, 1995, 1996, 2000, 2001, 2002. Used by permission of NavPress Publishing Group. All rights reserved.

Scripture quotations marked "CEV" are from the *Holy Bible; Contemporary English Version,* Copyright © 1995, Barclay M. Newman, ed., American Bible Society. Used by permission. All rights reserved.

The opinions expressed by the author are not necessarily those of Tate Publishing, LLC.

Published in the United States of America

ISBN: 978-1-6024723-6-5

07.05.07

For the Glory of God

Contents

Introduction

Children's ministry is a great place to be. It is full of life. It is fun and exciting and ever changing. What, it's not? Oh my! Well, it should be!

Today's kids have access to all things entertaining. From toys that practically do all the playing themselves to an unlimited supply of movies, kids are flooded with things that stimulate their senses in unbelievable ways.

When we were kids, children's ministry was much simpler than it needs to be today. Songs were sung, pictures were colored and stories were told, often with "flannel graph" or picture books. Here and there we would see an overhead transparency. Can you picture these methods having favorable results today?

Kids need to be engaged. Unfortunately, they need to be "Wowed." The stories in the Bible are very exciting and that needs to be conveyed in an exciting way. "Flannel graph" is not exciting and singing songs is only great if all of your kids know the songs they are singing and they have action in them.

If you are ready for an action-packed children's ministry experience, for the leaders and the kids, then this book is just the thing for you. If you do not agree that children's ministry needs to be exciting and that all that is required is to provide a little craft to go along with a Bible story then you need to put this book down immediately. The themes in this book are not for you if you do not desire to show the kids that learning about Jesus is fun.

The kids in your ministry will be left wanting more and more with these themes. They will return to each event wondering what you have up your sleeve for the next round. You will have no problem getting their attention because they will be excited to see how everything ties together.

You will find yourself having more fun at each event than you ever imagined. You will also find it easier to get volunteers to help you since they want to be part of the action as well.

2

So, You Want to Have a Thriving Ministry, huh?

Okay. You are interested in ministry that Leaves 'Em Wanting More!

You have a mission. You are leading a children's ministry—either for one session or for many. Either way, you have a very important job. You are being called upon to introduce Christ to kids—or enhance their knowledge of Christ in their lives. Can you think of any greater responsibility?

With such amazing stories to tell as the ones in the Bible it should be a breeze to get the kids to be interested. But, let's face it—kids just want to have fun! They go to school and have less and less fun as recess becomes shorter each year, or even non-existent. The curriculum requirements in school are more rigorous each year.

If your ministry is meeting on a weeknight you will likely have kids that just want to play with their friends. That is understandable but does not fit in with your mission. You need to get them engaged and participating in your activities and lead them into a discussion time that will be worthwhile.

To do that you need a few things that are the foundation of a thriving children's ministry:

* A leader with a heart and a mission for the spiritual well-being of the kids

* A dynamo—someone that will make things exciting and get the kids revved up.

* A great game leader.

* Support leaders that will be present and approachable among the kids and participate with them.

* A discussion leader that will talk to the kids in "kid-friendly" language

* Discipline and a disciplinarian that is fair, firm but not harsh and most of all—consistent.

* Patience

* Fun activities: lots of games that allow them to play and creative expression that provides hands-on learning

* Unpredictability—if the kids know what is going to happen before they even show up they will find something else to occupy their interests.

* Prayer!

Nobody expects you to do all of these things yourself. You will need to assemble a team of people that will do the best job to provide each of them. Some people can fill more than one role. People like that are amazing assets to your team and you need to utilize their abilities. People that fulfill only one role are equally important and should also be appreciated.

First of all is the leader with a passion for children's ministry. A warm body will not be sufficient in this role. There must be passion and the kids will need to see that, as well as the parents. Without passion it is just a bunch of activities. With passion there will be a lot of life in the ministry and the kids will know that they are loved and cared for.

Next is the dynamo. The dynamo will breathe a lot of life into your ministry. Having a few dynamos is great as they keep things fresh and always moving. They are wonderful for getting the kids excited and increasing the fun. They need to be among the kids, playing. Don't put a leash on them if they are in line with your ministry endeavors–allow them to flourish in the ministry. Let them know what is expected and what you are hoping to accomplish. With them "playing" you will see the kids having more fun because of their antics.

You will need a great game leader. Leading a game may sound like a piece of cake but it is not. You could be prepared to play the best game ever and it is no fun at all because the game leader wasn't enjoyable. A great game leader will:

* Separate into teams for the game with ease, hopefully creating teams of equal abilities.

* Explain the game and its rules in easily understandable language.

* Bring life to the game because they are excited about it.

* Enjoy refereeing the game as much or even more than playing it.

* Insist on fair play. (They should not be afraid to penalize a cheater or a rough player with a "time out" from play–the game needs to be fun for everyone!)

* Think on their feet and make adjustments to the game or the score if necessary.

* Insist that there is no arguing with the referee–this is important to keep the flow of activity. If debate is allowed you will have kids that argue every point. They can point out an issue of unfairness but be expected to drop it if the action they want is not taken.

You will need some support leaders. The role of these leaders is to offer maturity of presence. They are the eyes and ears throughout the group of kids. The up-front leader cannot see everything and deal with it personally, nor should they try to. To keep things moving and fresh you will need to rely on your support leaders to facilitate the best possible environment.

Next is a discussion leader, or leaders, that will talk to the kids in kid-friendly language while not talking down to them. The discussion should not be one-sided either. Kids need to be involved in the discussion. Ask them questions and allow them to ask questions.

Some kids will ask time-wasting or inappropriate questions. Don't be afraid to offer to answer those questions later, but allow them to ask them. You and your leaders may become frustrated with the amount of silly questions but allowing them to be asked will send a message to the kids that their questions are important. If you allow the silly ones but deal with them appropriately the kids will be more likely to ask the really important ones because they know they are important to you.

Patience is a key element. You are dealing with kids and they need to be allowed to be kids. That means noise, struggles to keep focused, immaturity, need for constant stimulation, lots of questions, the need to be seen and offered attention, and mess. The list could continue but you get the point. An amazing amount of patience will be necessary each time you come together as a group, especially if your group is large or you have any children that consistently challenge authority. Fortunately you are not alone and the most patient one, who is always willing to listen when you are frustrated, is just a prayer away.

Next are the fun activities. The themes and sessions in this book provide the blueprints. Your team makes the fun happen. The more fun you and your team have the more fun the kids will have and you will Leave 'Em Wanting More!

Along with the fun activities comes the unpredictability. The best games will be requested over and over again. Some of the best games you will play with them will be represented in multiple themes, when they fit into it well. Resist the urge to play the favorite games regularly. Even the best games will get old when they are played too often. Keep it fresh with new and exciting activities.

Being unpredictable goes beyond the activities though. Mixing things up with your methods of separating into teams, scorekeeping for games, leader participation in games, etc. will all enhance this part of your ministry.

As you look through the themes you will notice that there is an array of activities. Games, science experiments, craft projects and movie clips are all represented but aside from playing games in each session none of the other elements are incorporated in every theme. The purpose of that is to prevent routine.

Obviously some routine is necessary but the kids should be kept wondering what is coming next. Don't let them know anything ahead of time. Keep them guessing and don't divulge any secrets. Also, don't tell them the theme before the session begins. They will enjoy guessing what it is as the session unfolds.

There will be times when you need them to dress appropriately for the session, or bring something specific with them. You can accomplish this with a note home to parents prior to the session that requires this. In regard to dressing appropriately you should consider a note the first time you meet that covers everything. It could look like this:

We are happy your child is participating in our group. We plan to have a lot of fun with the kids in the sessions to come. Comfortable clothing and footwear for high levels of activity will be necessary for each session. While we don't want to give away any details ahead of time we do want to be responsible and make you aware that some of the activities could be wet, sticky or downright messy. Please don't allow your child to wear any clothing to a session that you would be concerned about having stained. Also, we recommend that you keep a towel in your vehicle for your child and something to protect it's upholstery on the way home - just in case.

Finally, and most importantly, your ministry will need lots of prayer. Allow God to use your ministry for His glory and commit each session, leader, child and parent to Him in prayer. If He is driving it the ministry will thrive!

3

How to Use These Themes

You have a prime opportunity! By selecting a curriculum based on a different theme for each session you are allowing for something brand new to take place each time your group of kids comes together. The kids are going to thrive on this approach and want to come back each time just to see what you could possibly come up with next.

Here are a few simple guidelines for using this theme-based curriculum:

1. Let them know that there will be a theme each time but you are not going to tell them what it is. Resist the urge to tell them the theme in advance at all costs. You will get a reputation for not divulging anything, which is great. It enables you to maintain control and keep things fresh.

    They will have a great time trying to guess what the theme is each time. Some of them will be obvious right from the start of the first activity, others will be a stretch but eventually they will figure it out. Some kids will begin guessing the moment they walk in the door and see something you have set up. You will have a blast keeping them in the dark and seeing how they come up with their guesses.

Some themes are generic and are based on something very typical, for instance, the "Air" theme. They may be surprised at how you can build a theme around something as simple as that. It will be exciting to see the theme unfold and, when you get one of those "Aha" moments you will be able to focus in on it and turn a theme into a wonderful teaching tool.

2. Offer specific opportunities to guess the theme as the evening unfolds. You will find that the one that guesses the theme correctly will feel good about him/her self even though there is no tangible prize involved in guessing the theme.

3. Be faithful to the theme. Try to work in the title of the theme as you are explaining a game. For example: During explanation of the games for the "Change" theme use language like, "We are going to play soccer, but with one major change . . ." or in the "Knock" theme, "Your goal is to knock your opponent off of the line . . ."

4. Be excited about each theme. The details are spelled out for you but it is only as good as the enthusiasm you bring to it. Don't be afraid to be loud and obnoxious, or, dare I say it… have FUN yourself. If you are having a good time the kids will too. You are allowed to have fun with them, and they will love it.

5. Be prepared. Don't go into the event having not read through the discussion. In most cases you will want to tweak it to your own style. Don't just stand there and merely read it out of this book. Storytelling is a lot of fun, but a storyteller needs to take ownership to the story and bring his or her own flavor to it.

6. If you LOVE it, they will come! Following the plans for each theme will provide for a great event. If you love it and put your heart into it you will provide for an AWESOME event. They will want to come back next time because they didn't get enough.

Parents will be thrilled to drop their child off next time and you will know that you have left them wanting more!

4

What's in Your Supply Closet?

You may already have a supply closet that has all the basics. If you are fortunate you have one that is fully stocked and you have everything you need for a fantastic event at your fingertips. Or, perhaps, you don't have much of anything at your disposal and you need to beg, borrow and steal to round up the things you need to put an event together. The key is to know what you have available—either in your supplies or through other resources that you can borrow from, and what you need to acquire to enhance your ministry.

Honestly, you can do a lot with very little. A few balls and other sports equipment, some simple craft items and a creative mind will suffice for many activities. But, if you really want to build a ministry that remains fresh and exciting there are some things you should consider adding to your arsenal.

Following is a list of supplies that you will find very helpful. Some are very basic and you can easily justify the expense. Others will take an activity from great to AWESOME or offer a "WOW" factor that will create quite a buzz and, of course, Leave 'Em Wanting More.

To make platform scooters:

Materials: 12" or 18" square x 1" thick wood
                     4 free rotation wheels with flanges
                     Screws for flanges

Attach wheels at corners of platform 1" from edges.

General Needs	Sports Equipment	Craft Items	Toys/Games
-Whistle	-Balls — variety of types ranging from ping-pong to kickballs. Be sure to have plenty of soft foam balls for dodgeball games.	-Scissors — many pairs	-Pool Noodles
-Stopwatch (a few will be handy)		-Glue	-Kiddie Pools
-Masking tape in various colors	-Platform scooters — several. These can be purchased or made by a handy volunteer.	-Paper	-Hula-Hoops (several)
-Cones		-Fluorescent paint	
-CD Player	See instructions in this section.	-Tempera Paint	
-Buckets	-Wiffle ball bats	-Embroidery Floss	
-Kid Friendly Bible	-Batting tee	-Markers—various types of washable and permanent	
-TV	-Razor scooters		
-VCR	-Giant ball—"Bigens" is one brand name of ball that comes in up to 50" sizes. It takes a while to inflate but can be deflated for storage if you don't have room to keep it stored. If you have room to store it you will appreciate the ability to pull it out and use it in a pinch. One of the best games you will play is "Change-Up Dodgeball" (see closing activity for "Change", also called "Out of Control Dodgeball" and is an alternate closing activity for the session with the same theme) and it is best with a big ball. This is a great addition to your supplies!	-Pencils	
-DVD Player		-Paint brushes or Q-tips	
-Tape Layer (if your facility does not have lines on the floor for you to work with easily)			
	-Carpet Skates (if your facility is carpeted) — several pairs		
	-Inflatable pool rings (at least 2)		
	-Pinneys		
	-Batting Tee		
	-Bases		
	-Jump Ropes		
	-Goals (if you don't have actual goals you can use laundry baskets)		
	-Something to serve as a volleyball net		

5

Housekeeping For Your Ministry

The themes in this book are fresh and exciting. Executing them to their full potential will require some basic skills to be mastered. The cleanest house will still get dusty if left alone. The same is true with a thriving ministry. Some attention to details will make things run smoothly and keep things simple. Some things mentioned here might seem elementary to you but consider that some of us called into children's ministry do not think along the lines of the details because we just want to have fun and offer the message of God's love. That's great, but without attention to some basic elements you will have chaos and frustration and won't even get to the heart of your mission.

If you are confident that you can handle all of the things covered here then feel free to ignore this chapter. Even better, tear it out of the book all together. Be careful though, you may have a substitute some night that desperately needs this instruction and you might not find those pages again. Just in case you may want to purchase another copy of this book to put in the hands of substitutes as that need arises.

Rules

Everyone hates rules but they are absolutely necessary, especially when working with a large group of kids. You need to be concerned with safety as well as maintaining an environment that provides the best opportunity for the kids to grow and learn. In order to do so you need to have clear expectations for their behavior.

Establish clear safety rules at the beginning and be prepared to enforce them. You will also need to discipline kids who don't follow the rules of the games. Your goal is to provide a place where the kids can come and have a great time. It is not fun when kids are cheating. Keep an eye on it and give stern warnings to offenders. Follow up ignored warnings by making errant kids sit out of a game. The games are so much fun that they will respond very well to this form of punishment—even if they are the most challenging kid. The most important thing is to be consistent!

One of the most important rules you should have during the games is that there is no arguing with the referee. This will enable you to make a call and the play to continue regardless of who disagrees. Play the games with the authority that umpires and officials have in sports. Yes, you will make an unfair call. The kids can point it out calmly and you can change your mind if necessary, but do not allow arguments. That interrupts the flow and does nothing for the fun.

All other rules are at your discretion. Don't have too many rules though. That prevents them from just being kids and having fun.

Breaking into teams

Each session will require you to separate into teams. This is a mundane procedure but you will need to accomplish it quickly and efficiently. Some people like to make this into a game. That's a great idea and should be considered each time it fits into the theme.

There are some easy ways to accomplish this efficiently. Think back to all those gym classes when you were a kid. The easiest way is to have all the kids line up, shoulder to shoulder, with their toes on a line, all facing the same direction. You may need to put a line down with tape if your facility does not have one. Then it's a matter of counting off by whatever number you need or choose. This gets the job done quickly, though you should consider a few things:

1. Some kids will manipulate the teams by pre-counting and positioning themselves to make sure they have the same number as the friends they want to be on the same team with.

2. You can easily end up with uneven teams. There are times that the ability of a team is not a factor in the game but it can also mean the difference in how much fun a game is if the teams are unevenly matched.

Another easy way to do this is to have them find a partner, or as many partners necessary for the number of teams you want. Example: two teams, they get one partner; three teams, they get two partners. They will most likely choose people of similar ability to theirs, or the person that they cannot be separated from. Once they have their partners tell them each to choose a number. Then designate the teams as 1's, 2's and so on. Be prepared for grumbles and groans from the ones that can't bear to be separated from their partners and use your discretion with making exceptions. Typically they can stand to be separated for some games and usually they are happy to compete against each other.

At times when ability is not a factor in playing the game or the activity allow them to choose who they want to be with, making sure the groups are evenly numbered.

Scoring of games

Whenever there is a game there is an objective in mind. There are rare times when simply playing the game is the objective. Typically, though, the game results in a winner and loser. Games are way more fun if the competition is close, so do whatever you can to ensure that if it does not happen naturally. This may mean fixing the score a bit. Don't lie about it—just find creative ways to keep it close. This would be invoking the "Scorekeeper's Allowance."

You can keep the score close very simply by offering random bonus points for demonstrations of strong character. Examples are: good sportsmanship; helpfulness; encouragement; creativity; good attitude and any other good quality you want to enforce. Don't be afraid to dole out the points here and there. There is nothing wrong with that. If they argue, remind them of the rule that states, "No Arguing With the Referee!" If they continue, offer points to the team that is not arguing. Continue to do so until the arguing stops.

You can also offer assistance to kids that are struggling. Kids are perceptive enough to see that you are trying to keep it even and allow everyone to participate and have a good time, and that is something you want to foster.

The best way to determine a winner in "relay" games and provide for transition to your next activity is to stipulate that the team that not only finishes the race first, but also is sitting quietly when the race is done first, is the winner. This works great because it then doesn't come down to the team that just finished first. It allows all teams to complete the race and then still qualify for bragging rights, simply based on behavior. They will catch on quickly too when the race is over and you wait for quiet to declare the winner. How shocking it will be when the winner is not the team that accomplished the task first but that focused their attention quietly first.

Discussion

The discussions are written out for you within each theme. They can get rather lengthy and you don't want to just read them from this book. Copy them and put them inside your Bible and read them from there instead, or just jot down the points to keep you moving as you relay the story in your own words.

Video clips are a great visual to tie into your discussion. Whenever possible show one to set the stage or during the discussion to further emphasize a point. There are many suggested within the details of the discussion but use something different if you know it fits better or is more appropriate for your specific group of kids than what is included in the curriculum details.

Another element to consider is the use of a candy quiz to wrap up your discussion. There is no reference to one in any particular theme but could be a welcomed addition to any evening, particularly one with a concept you want to really drive home. If they know it is coming they will also pay closer attention during your story.

A candy quiz is very simple. After you complete your story you will quiz them to see how well they listened. You will need to have a bag, hat, basket or other container with candy in it and just ask random questions of the group. Insist kids raise their hands to answer the question and then toss them a piece of candy when they answer it correctly. Then move on to the next question quickly. Keep it moving and lively and try to get each kid to answer at least one question, asking a real simple one if necessary for some kids.

Now, the house is clean. Time to move on to the fun stuff! Themes are in alphabetical order, not in the order you should execute them.

Air

Theme Target:
Teach kids that they blow it when they sin, but God forgives when they ask.

Golden Nugget:
Don't blow it!

Scripture:
David & Bathsheba 2 Samuel 11–12 (NIV)

Instruct the kids ahead of time to wear old clothes and shoes—perhaps even bring an old towel to help clean themselves up.

Activity #1: Frisbee Basketball or Football

Throw a Frisbee through a hula-hoop goal—either suspended from something or held up by leaders. Play with normal Basketball rules otherwise. Instead of dribbling they must throw the Frisbee. Also, they are not allowed to run with the Frisbee.

For added fun the target can move if a leader is holding it up.

Activity #2: Balloon Relay

Split into teams–you decide how many based on number of kids. Each team or each kid, your choice, gets one balloon–a small one. On "Go" they blow up their balloons and then, kid at the head of the line starts moving toward the cone at the other end of the playing area. They must keep their balloon up in the air at all times, by blowing on it. Be prepared to demonstrate this. They go around a cone and back to their line. If they drop their balloon they must pick it up, take three steps back and start from there.

The first team to finish and is also sitting quietly wins the game. It's a great idea that you insist they be quiet when all teams are done and determine the winner based on their silence at that point. They will catch on after you've scored the winner this way a few times and it helps to get control for the transition to the next activity.

Activity #3: Balloon Volleyball

Play volleyball with a sixteen-inch balloon or larger. Give up to five hits per side if you find they need it. If you have lots of kids you could have them be on their knees or sitting. It prevents them from crowding each other out. For added fun put a little bit of weight in the balloon–a coin or two work well; so does a little bit of water. It causes the balloon to shift a bit during flight and adds an unexpected element that is fun and if you use a bit of water it's a lot of fun to see who gets it if it pops.

If you don't have a volleyball net here are a few alternate suggestions:

* If the kids sit you can use a row of chairs, set side by side like musical chairs. It helps to block their view–a new twist on the game.

* A rope or pennant flag duct taped or attached to the wall in some way. You can attach items to the rope with clothespins so the kids can see it better.

* Room dividers can be fun because it makes them pay close at-

tention since they won't know where the balloon is coming from before it clears the top.

Activity #4: Air Painting simultaneous with Air Wars

Air Painting–needs to be done outside or somewhere with good ventilation and substantial dropcloth or newspaper protection. If you are concerned with potential mess to clothing provide smocks to protect from paint splatter. USE TEMPERA PAINT to provide for wash ability. Depending on your budget or what you have access to there are a few ways to accomplish this:

Low budget: Give the kids a few balloons each. Put your paint in squeeze bottles. They then carefully squeeze a little bit of paint into their balloon and then blow it up, tight but not so it pops on them. Once they have their paint balloons full they lay their paper on the drop cloth, hold the balloon above it, and then pop it with a pushpin. The paint will splatter differently each time. Be careful–it will really splatter depending on its liquid consistency–but this is some serious fun!

Budget with some frills: Provide BloPens to paint their pictures with. These are a bit more expensive than markers and definitely don't last as long, but they are a lot of fun. BEWARE: Use outside if possible. Tape newspaper or dropcloth to wall and then tape the paper to the wall too.

These things are great but imagine what happens in an enclosed area, with a bunch of kids leaning over a table with a piece of paper on it, blowing hard into something that then sprays marker ink onto the paper intending to make it splatter. Tables are usually only a few feet wide and anyone would naturally think that you could allow the kids on both sides, right? Take it from me, you don't want to do this; I nearly gave a room full of people respiratory distress. But the things are really cool and the kids love them!

Bells & Whistles: If you have access to air brushes you can give each kid a temporary tattoo. You also need an air source–air compressor, canned air or, believe it or not, spare tires. You also need someone that knows how these things work and how to troubleshoot problems. Have one or two stencils to choose from and only allow them one color on their tattoo—then you only need one color per airbrush. Your leader's could do their tattoo or they could pair up and paint a temporary tattoo on their partner's arm or vice versa. Once everything is set up it's really simple for the kids to do and it would be exciting for them to be the tattoo artist. You could make a cool stencil—print out a logo on card stock, then cut it out with an exacto knife—with the theme's application, like this one:

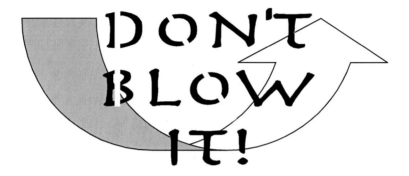

Instructions for a temporary tattoo:

* ★ Wipe arm clean with an alcohol swab.
* ★ Position the stencil and airbrush it.
* ★ Dab some baby powder on it with a pad or brush and leave it on for five minutes to "set" it.

Simultaneously with the painting play Air Wars:

This also has a few budget tracks:

Low budget: The old tie a balloon around your ankle and see how long you can protect it from being popped. Or do the "Budget with frills" option, if you have access to leaf blowers. This can also be done with a small, handheld, battery-operated fan–but it's not as cool (pardon the pun: Fan–Cool). Do not use a hair dryer, it will quickly overheat and the cord is a tripping hazard.

Budget with Frills: Borrow or rent two leaf blowers and do a relay. Each team has a leaf blower and they use it to, one by one, blow a ball down and around a cone and hand off to the next kid. Or, you could play steal the bacon or line hockey and they either blow the ball, or other "blowable" item across their line or into a goal while someone from the other team is attempting to do the same thing.

Bells & Whistles: If you have access to a small, two person moon bounce or decide to rent one or have it donated for the evening, set it up and allow the pairs of two to play for two minutes or until the game is over.

Break up into two teams and match up the kids of either equal size or skill and have them go head to head in combat. You could do a belt with flags or clothespins on it, like flag football. On "GO" each kid protects their flags by moving around, while also trying to take the other ones flags.

There is a great combat game on the market that works very well for this. It is called "Combat" and consists of two battery-powered armbands with a timer and sensor. You set the timer on them and they keep track of how many times they have had contact made with them during the time. Each kid puts one on his/her arm and you push the "Start" button. They each then try to tap the other one's band, while protecting their own. It beeps at the end of the timer and you get the kids out of the moon bounce and check to see which one got more shots in.

Discussion: What happens when you blow it?

Stage a "Jerry Springer" like interview with the kids as the audience. You will need an adult male to play "David" and an interviewer. For an added touch you could have a gorgeous woman play Bathsheba and someone play Uriah–but you could get away without these actors and David could hold up a photo of a very beautiful woman.

You are the host of a talk show and your kids are the audience. Instruct a few of your leaders, who are sitting amongst the kids, to participate in the interview by "booing" David or heckling him as he describes his sin.

For your set-up of this discussion:

Place a chair on your "stage." You should also have a few index cards with your questions on them, to keep it going. A few of your leaders in the audience should have questions for "David" as well. If the kids are into it you can allow them to ask questions as well–use your own judgment on that one.

Here's the script.

Players
Discussion Leader = DL
David
Audience Member 1 = AM1
Audience Member 2 = AM2
Audience Member 3 = AM3

DL: Welcome to "They Blew It" the talk show that brings you all the juiciest stories of people that have really blown it by their actions. We dish you the dirt and you decide their fate.

Our guest today is a very prominent man. He is actually a government official–King of Israel. His name is David and he is known as a very good man. It has been written that he is a "man after God's own heart." That's a pretty impressive description for a guy appearing on this show. We usually get the lowest of the low as guests for this show but today, we bring you a guy that really knew better than to do what he did.

He had all the advantages in life. He was respected. He was wealthy—of course he was, he was a king. Let's bring him out here. Come on out David!

<David enters and sits down. AM1–3, plus any additional leaders, should be applauding and cheering for David–trying to get the kids to join in. David should be dressed like a king–if a modern-day king he should be in a nice suit and be wearing lots of jewelry. If a Bible-times king he should be in a bright-white, toga-like outfit with an ornate sash and something to resemble a crown. You should choose, based on your group of kids, which look will be more engaging for them. >

DL: Welcome to the show your highness.

David: Thank you very much. I'm happy to be here to share my story.

DL: Should I call you "your highness?"

David: You may call me King David. That is how I am referred to in all the stories about me.

DL: Okay. So, King David...Let's start with your background. Your father wasn't a king so how did you become King of Israel.

David: You're right. My father was a shepherd. You don't get much further from royalty than that. I became King because God chose me for that role. He anointed me himself.

DL: Didn't that cause a stir in the royal family–having an outsider take over the throne?

David: Who is going to argue with you when God himself has anointed you to become king and the king before you and his sons have just died?

DL: So, God chose you for king. Why was that?

David: God chose me because He loved me and I loved Him. Many people say I was a man who sought after God with all my heart. God gave me all my strength, power and courage.

DL: Tell us about the time when you didn't seek God with all your heart.

David: I guess that's why I'm here, so, here goes.

DL: I was already King and as King you get a lot of cool stuff. You run everything and everyone looks up to you and serves you. That was great but not what I was in it for. I had a job to do and I wanted to do it well.

David: Yeah, yeah–get to the part where you turned your back on God.

AM1:   Yeah–tell us how you sinned!

David: Well, I'm not proud of it at all. It's not easy to share. It was the lowest time in my life. I had always tried to be so good—to do what was expected of me and be a good example.

DL: (Taunting) But you still failed didn't you David?

David: (With head down) Yes, I did.

DL: You didn't just fail though. You broke a specific commandment from God, didn't you?

AM1–3:   (React shocked)

AM2:   Tell us what ya' did!

AM3:   Yeah–air your dirty laundry!

DL: Go ahead King David. Tell the audience how the wonderful, respectable, mighty King sinned against the same God that loved him and appointed him King.

David: Well, I saw this woman…this beautiful woman. The most beautiful woman I had ever seen. Instantly I wanted her for my own. But I couldn't have her. That caused me to want her even more.

DL: But you are the King. You can have any woman you want. And you already did have many wives. Why couldn't you have this woman?

David: She was already married–to a soldier in my army.

AM1: That didn't stop you though, did it?

David: (Puts his head in his hands) No. I sent for her anyway. I committed adultery with her.

AM2: Shame on you. You knew better!

David: I know. You don't know how badly I had to have her.

DL: That's not the end of the story is it King David?

David: No. I wish it were.

DL: Continue.

David: I found out she was pregnant with my child.

AM3: Shocking!

DL: You didn't confess to her husband either, did you?

David: No, I should have. But I didn't.

DL: What did you do?

AM2: He probably made it worse by trying to cover it up!!

David: (Stands up forcefully and points to heckler) You weren't there! You have no idea what was going through my head.

DL: Calm down King David. Just tell us what happened. We all want to know. (Turns to audience) Am I right?

David: I called her husband in to speak with me. I told him to go home and relax and spend time with his wife.

DL: You were hoping that he would go home to her and she would seduce him, then he would think the baby was his, weren't you?

David: (Pacing, with head down) Yes! That would have fixed everything.

DL: Is that what happened?

David: No! (In a mocking tone) Her husband was too loyal to his fellow troops. He stayed at the palace on guard duty. He never went home to her. He refused to leave his post to go and spend time with his wife if the rest of his troop couldn't go home.

DL: So you needed a new plan.

David: (With a bit of pride in voice) And I came up with one too. I had to take care of this, quickly.

AM1: (In a taunting tone) You killed the poor guy didn't you?

David: Come up here and say that, I dare you!

DL: King David, calm down. Just tell us what happened.

David: I sent her husband to battle and ordered that he be placed on the front line.

DL: That's not all though.

David: I instructed the leader of the army to have all the other troops with him to fall back–leaving him all alone to face the enemy.

DL: You knew what would happen to him didn't you?

David: Duh!

DL: So, with her husband dead you could send for her to come to the palace and be your next wife. Then, it would be perfectly normal that she be pregnant with your child.

AM2: You should have had your crown taken!

David: You don't know me and you have no right to judge me.

DL: But, King David…you have to admit, this is pretty bad stuff that you did.

David: I know. I was so ashamed. I had sinned against God. I turned my back on Him with these actions.

DL: So–you were stripped of your throne then?

David: No.

DL: Everyone found out and you were humiliated then?

David: That wouldn't have mattered. It was bad enough to know what I had done.

DL: God took everything from you though, right?

David: No. The baby died when he was a week old and that was very sad. But I still had my new wife and God blessed us with another child, a boy, and God loved him very much.

DL: Why would God bless you after you sinned against Him in this way? He should have taken everything from you and sent you back to being a shepherd. Did you make a deal with Him? Did you have to serve the poor or clean out animal stalls or something?

David: No, none of those things.

DL: Then, what could you have possibly done that would cause God to forgive you, allow you to remain King, and even bless you and this woman that you sinned with by giving you a child that He loved?

David: I prayed to God and told Him I was sorry for all of the things I had done to sin against Him.

<Pause>

DL: That's it? That's all you did?

David: That's all God requires. He forgave me immediately when I asked Him to.

DL: But you really blew it!

David: I know.

DL: So, you want us to believe that you did all those things with your back turned away from God and when you went to Him and said you were sorry He just forgave you?

David: That's right. God loves me. He was very unhappy with me for the things I did. I knew that. I was truly sorry and when I told Him that He forgave me completely. That's how God works–for me and for everyone else that loves Him.

DL: *(To audience)* There you have it! God forgives us when we sin, if we are sorry and ask Him to.

Final activity: Air Bubble

This is a good old bubble-blowing contest. Give each kid one or two pieces of bubble gum. On "GO" they unwrap their gum and begin chewing it as quickly as possible. When able they blow a bubble. The first one to blow a bubble wins the game. Continue for a few minutes to see who can blow the largest bubble within the time frame you specify.

Supplies Needed for "Air" Based on Funds available			
Activity	Budget	Budget w/ some frills	Bells & Whistles
Frisbee Basketball or Football	-Frisbee -2 Hula-hoops -Cones for boundaries -Pinneys	Same	Same
Balloon Relay	-Balloons -Cones	Same	Same
Balloon Volleyball	-16" or large balloon -Volleyball Net -Cones	Same	Same
Air Painting	-Dropcloth, newspaper or plastic -Tempera paint -Balloons -Paper -Pushpins	-Blopens -Paper -WELL VENTILATED AREA -Stencils -Pencils	-Airbrush(es) -Water based paint safe for skin, thinned to spraying consistency -Air supply – compressor; canned air; spare tire(s) -Stencil(s) -Alcohol -Cotton balls or pads -Baby powder -Large Cosmetic Brush or soft bristled paint brush -Dropcloth if not outside -Table

Air Wars	-String, yarn or rubber bands -Balloons	-2 Leaf blowers or handheld, battery-operated fans -Ball or balloon -Masking tape for boundary lines or 2 laundry baskets or 2 hockey goals	-Moon bounce -2 belts with flags or clothespins or -"Combat" game -Stopwatch
Air Bubble	Bubble gum	Same	Same

Bubble

Theme Target:
Teach kids how to clean their heart.

Golden Nugget:
Jesus' blood cleans up our sins!

Scripture:
Hebrews 9:22 (NIV)

In fact, the law requires that nearly everything be cleansed with blood and without the shedding of blood there is no forgiveness.

For this event kids should have been warned ahead of time to wear old clothes, bring a towel and a change of clothes. They will get very wet–so save this for a nice weather event.

Activity #1: Frozen Bubble (approximately ten minutes)

Freeze enough bubblegum, in the wrapper, for one per kid. For added fun for the leaders use that gum that is so sour it makes you cry. Remove from freezer just before playing.

"In this game you will each be given a piece of bubble gum. On "GO" you will open it and chew it as fast as you can. The first five kids to blow a bubble with their gum will win the game."

You don't need a prize here. Bragging rights or the gum they are now chewing is their prize.

Activity #2: Bubble Kickball

Play as long as they are having fun. For the amount of prep you should get a good amount of time out of it, but be sensitive to kids that get too cold.

This is kickball with an enormous twist. All of the bases except home plate are kiddie pools full of water and bubbles. Use Baby Shampoo for the bubbles so it doesn't hurt eyes when splashed in face. Base path between 3rd base and home plate can be clear plastic with Baby shampoo on it for bubbles. For this you will need water supply to keep it slick and bubbly–either a hose or a sprayer with water in it. This element is not necessary but is a ton of fun if you do it.

Regular kickball rules apply except runner must have both feet in the pool to be safe.

Don't play three outs and they switch offense to defense. Bat (kick) through the batting order and then count only the runs that scored. If they get out they stand on one side, if they score a run they stand on the other. This allows everyone to play.

If your baby pool is big enough for multiple kids in there you can have a rule that does not require them to advance to the next base unless there are more than two kids in that base already.

Activity #3: Bubble explosion & Bubble Painting

If you have leaders enough to run both of these activities simultaneously it keeps the kids better occupied.

Bubble Explosion

Make your bubble solutions ahead of time–this stuff works great and can be stored in a closed container for a long time. It just gets better and better with time.

Bubble recipe:

 * 2 cups Dawn dish detergent–original formula
 * 1 gallon plus 2 cups water
 * 1 cup glycerin (available in Pharmacies) or light corn syrup–don't use syrup if there are bees near where you will be doing this activity though

Pour your bubble solution into a kiddie pool.

Provide lots of bubble blowing items for the kids to blow an array of bubbles. More and more bubble blowing items are available all the time–so do some that are little and some really big.

Kids can make their own bubble wands.

Cut a string about two to three feet long. Pull the string through two non-bendable straws. Tie the string in a knot, and hide the knot inside a straw. By putting their hands on the straws and pulling, they create a square or rectangle. Dip this form into the pool of bubble solution, and gently draw it through the air. Voila, a giant bubble.

The hula-hoop will provide the ability for giant bubbles. It also would allow you to put a kid in a bubble. Put a stool in the middle of the hula-hoop in the kiddie pool of bubble solution and have a kid stand on it. Slowly raise the hula-hoop up around the kid. In the right weather conditions this will work great and is really cool for the kid. If it is too windy it will blow against the kid and pop. Provide a pair of goggles to protect eyes from the sting of a big popping bubble spray.

There is a product on the market called "Bubble Thing." With it the kids can make really long bubbles. The claim is that it will make bubbles as long as a bus but weather conditions have to be right. It won't work well on a windy day, and a bit humid is better. I highly recommend it because it is seriously cool!

Bubble Painting

* Put paint into painting containers–pie plate or cake pan size. Mix ¼ cup baby shampoo with each color of tempera paint you choose. Thin with water to stretch paint further.

* Each kid gets a straw.

* They blow into the paint to get it to bubble up.

* Lay paper on bubbles, but not down hard enough to reach paint reservoir.

Discussion:

You are going to do an object lesson that involves dye and bleach. Do not wear anything that you care about! PLEASE PRACTICE THIS OBJECT LESSON PRIOR TO THE EVENT TO MAKE SURE YOU HAVE THE DYE AND WATER PROPORTIONS WORKED OUT!

For this object lesson you will need them all to sit on the floor so they can see the table that you are working on. Don't let them come too close to the table. You don't want them to get splashed with bleach.

On the table you will need a clear, glass container, preferably round, and with sides. A fish bowl works great. In the bottom of that container you need to tape a pin or thumbtack–so that it is sticking up and will easily pop a water balloon when it is dropped into the water. Put a little bit of WARM clear water in the bottom, not too much but enough that it can be seen on the sides.

In a non see-through container you will need several water balloons that are filled with water that has black die in it. Use only enough dye to make the water black enough to represent sin. Do not use straight dye.

In the same container you will have one water balloon that is filled with pure bleach–do not water down the bleach. This should be a red balloon, the only red balloon. You will need to keep this balloon at room temperature. If it gets too warm it will burst before you are ready and too cold, it may not work right.

This bowl that I have here is clear and round. We'll use that to represent your life. Notice that it has clean water in it. This clean water represents the image in which you are created. God made you, and He does not make mistakes.

Unfortunately, you are human, and humans are not perfect like God is. Ever since the first humans, Adam and Eve, sinned, we have all had that sin nature in us. So, I need to add the sin nature to this. <Drop in a dye balloon–make sure you drop it in hard enough that it pops, but minimize the splash.>

Just like that, you are black from sin.

Since you are human you sin, and sin and sin. <Drop in a dye balloon every time you emphasize this>

Now look at you. You are completely black from sin. That's pretty different than the nice clean image of God, isn't it? Because you are black from sin you are not able to join God in Heaven. Only those who are clean may go to Heaven. But we all want to go to Heaven. And God wants you there more than anything. So, He gave Jesus to make that possible. <Pull out the red bleach balloon>

Jesus died on the cross to take away our sins. <Drop in the bleach balloon> *His blood covered our sin for us. But we are still black until we accept Jesus.* <At this point the black is clearing or is clear all together. The water doesn't go completely clear though> *His blood is there for us and when we accept Him into our hearts and lives He takes away that black sin and leaves His blood there in it's place. The Bible tells us that blood is required for forgiveness and cleansing to take place.*

We have been cleaned of our sins completely and now we try to live right and do what is pleasing to God. Unfortunately, we don't always choose right and we still sin now and then. <Drop in another dye balloon>

The sin that we commit doesn't make God happy and we know that. But we know that God loves us and fortunately Jesus is still there. He always will be there. <The water should be clearing again, or should be clear already> *His blood will always be stronger than the sin and will always cover it.*

This is a perfect opportunity to offer an invitation to accept Jesus. You need to be ready to offer one at anytime it is appropriate, and you need to be extremely comfortable with the words you use to share it. If you have not done so already prepare, in your own words, the words for your invitation. Remember, it needs to be simple for kids to understand, sincere in its tone and succinct in its delivery. For an example of an invitation you will find one in the "Salvation Invitation" section of this book.

If anyone accepts your invitation and asks Jesus into their heart for the first time please make it a special celebration with the rest of the group. It's not a time for embarrassment but they should be aware of their awesome step of faith. Tell them that there is a party in Heaven at that moment for the place that has been reserved for them!

Closing Activity: Bubble Wrap Challenge

Split into as many teams as you have bubble wrap for. This is a relay race. Teams wrap one player at a time in bubble wrap–keep hands to side–and then tie a belt around their waist. Once "wrapped" player waddles down and around a cone and back to their team, which helps unwrap them and wraps next player.

The first team to get everyone done, get the bubble wrap re-rolled or folded and **is sitting quietly,** wins the game.

Supplies Needed for "Bubble" Based on Funds available			
Activity	Budget	Budget w/ some frills	Bells & Whistles
Frozen Bubble	-Bubble gum – 1 piece per kid	Same	Same
Bubble Kickball	-3 kiddie pools that can fit at least one kid in. -Water to fill the kiddie pool at least ½ way -3 bottles Baby shampoo -Kickball	Same but with 6 bottles of Baby shampoo instead	Same but add -Clear plastic to line base path -Hose to keep base paths wet and bubbly -Kickball

Bubble explosion	-Buckets of homemade bubble solution – see recipe instructions above	-Same plus "Bubble Thing"	Same plus a Bubble Machine
	-Kiddie pool – can dump out one of others and use it		
	-Assortment of Bubble making objects		
	-Straws		
	-Cotton yarn		
	-Hula-hoop		
Bubble painting	-Pie tins or cake pans	Same	Same
	-Tempera paint		
	-Dishwashing liquid		
	-Straws		
	-Water		
	-Paper		
	-Goggles		
Discussion	-Bible	Same	Same
	-Fish bowl – or other round, clear, glass container		
	-Water		
	-Pin or thumbtack – taped to bottom of bowl		
	-Water balloons		
	-Black dye		
	-Bleach		
	-Bucket or other non see-through container		
	-Table		
	-White towel		
Bubble wrap challenge	-Bubble Wrap	Same	Same
	-Cones		
	-Belt		

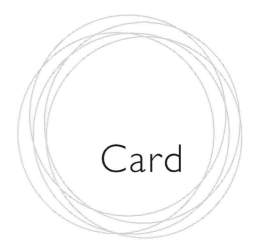

Card

Theme Target:

Teach kids about the payment that Christ made for them or teach them about having a foundation in Christ versus in the world.

Golden Nugget:

The cross is the ultimate credit card or, What is your life built on?

Scripture:

Either Romans 6:23 (NIV) For the wages of sin is death, but the gift of God is eternal life in Christ Jesus our Lord. or Matthew 7: 24–27 (NIV) Therefore everyone who hears these words of mine and puts them into practice is like a wise man who built his house on the rock. The rain came down, the streams rose, and the winds blew and beat against that house; yet it did not fall, because it had its foundation on the rock. But everyone who hears these words of mine and does not put them into practice is like a foolish man who built his house on sand. The rain came down, the streams rose, and the winds blew and beat against that house, and it fell with a great crash.

For this event you will play some good old favorites with a twist. You will choose the teams by using cards.

Before the event begins put a pack of playing cards in the order you want to break up in teams by. Example: Alternate black and red cards, with the suits mixed up though. Kill two birds with one stone and order them by number as well–so that when you give them out you will have the teams designated and then, among their teams, small kids will have small numbers and the numbers get progressively larger according to kid.

At the beginning of the event have all the kids line up in one long line, by order of size—smallest to tallest—in the area you designate (I like to use a line and have them put their toes on it). You will then give each kid a playing card. They will hang on to that playing card all night. That card will be what determines their place in the "lineup" for each activity.

Activity #1: Catch Me if You Can

(you could call it something else to match the theme, like "Card tag" or "Card Scramble" or something like that, if you like to have the name match the theme).

Put a line of masking tape down the center of the room.

Instruct the members of the largest team to get a chair and bring it to the center of the room. You will create a line of chairs, set up like musical chairs with them alternating the direction they face. There should also be one and one half chair widths in between each of them. Leave as much room as possible at the ends of the line without crowding your chairs too close. Finally, take away one chair, so there is one for each team member minus one (the remaining player is the chaser).

The other team is to line up against the wall, according to their card order–you decide whether it's low to high or vice versa. Also, decide what value Ace will have, either lowest or highest. The kid at the front of the line is the first runner.

It should look like this:

LINE OF WAITING RUNNERS

LOCATION TO SIT WHEN TAGGED

The team in the chairs is "it" while the other team is being chased, one at a time.

Instruct the team that got the chairs to sit down on them, keeping their feet in **front** of the chair–an important safety rule to prevent a fall from accidental or intentional–(if intentional, discipline is necessary) tripping. Select one member to be the first runner by the card he or she is holding. For example, "Everyone sit on a chair, except for the four of clubs. You are the first chaser."

Now for the tricky part… We'll start with the team being chased.

The team that is being chased will release one player at a time. That player can run anywhere in the playing court–around the ends of the chairs, through the gaps between the chairs and anywhere on either side. The rest of the team stays in their line, waiting for their turn to run. Those waiting must keep one foot against the wall at all times (this is for safety purposes as it keeps them close to the wall. Trust me the line will drift away from the wall so the kids can see what is going on. This cuts down on the running space and creates safety issues).

The kid that is being chased runs as long as possible without being tagged by the other team's runner. Once tagged the chaser immediately goes to work on catching the next runner. The next runner needs to begin running immediately so they have a better chance of getting away. A leader will need to stand at the head of the line and watch for the runner to get tagged and notify the next runner to "GO." The team being chased must pay attention so they are ready for their turn. Also, the runner being chased needs to make sure they do not get tagged close to the rest of their team. If tagged too close to the line the chaser can easily go right down the line tagging each new player before they even get a chance to run.

Once tagged instruct the players that they are out and must sit or stand against the wall on the other side of the room.

The team that is "It" must only have one person running at a time, that runner is the chaser. Unfortunately, the chaser can only chase on one side of the chair line. If the runner crosses the line, either by running around it on either end or by running through it in a gap between chairs, the chaser must tap the shoulder of one of his teammates that is sitting in a chair facing the side that the runner is now on. The chaser cannot cross over the line. Once a new chaser is tapped and leaves their chair the retired chaser sits in the now empty seat and waits to be tapped again.

Keep a stopwatch running during each round. The team that lasts longer without all being tagged wins the round. The kids will want to play several rounds.

If this is the first time you are playing this game there are two important things to do:

1. Run the first round slowly so the kids get the hang of it. It may take the entire first round for them to remember to only run on their side, to use the gaps in the chairs, to not run full steam if it is not necessary (I have seen savvy kids eat up lots of time by not running much at all but, rather, just staying close to the chair line and crossing over far enough to be out of reach—utilizing the rule for chasers to not cross over).

2. Realize that this will not be the last time you play this game.

Be aware that you may use a lot of time explaining this game. It is difficult to explain without using examples, but once the kids know how to play it is a blast and will surely become a favorite.

Activity #2: Line Body Ball (if a giant ball) or Line Soccer

(again, you could change the name to fit the theme if you like—"Card Shark" seems fun)

Each team lines up on their goal line (use masking tape if you have no painted lines in your facility)–put cones at the ends of the line to create boundaries. Place the ball in the center of the playing court or field. When you call out a number the kid on either team that is holding the card with that number runs out and attempts to get the ball over the other team's line. The kids still on the line are responsible to block the ball to prevent the score. The line can send the ball back into play but cannot score by kicking it through the other team's line.

If the ball is a giant one the kids can use their whole body to move the ball. If it is a soccer or kick ball then only their feet can be used. The line can use any part of their body to block a goal and can kick or throw it back into play.

Once a goal is scored the players return to their lines. The ball is replaced in the center and you call the next number.

You determine the following during play:

1. If a ball is too high to be scored as a goal.

2. If the round is taking too long and additional numbers need to be called to speed up the scoring process.

3. Whether additional balls need to be added during a round of play–this can be great fun if a kid is left out or scoring is uneven.

Activity #3: Build Card Houses

Instruct the kids to get into groups–you decide how many in a group based on the number of kids and packs of cards–three kids or two kids and a leader works well for this. Give each group a pack or two of playing cards–depending on how many you have. Tell them each group will build a card house in a specified period of time–but don't tell them how much time. When you blow the whistle they begin to build and when you blow the whistle again all building must stop. Based on how well they participate you determine how long to continue this activity.

Know ahead of time whether you will allow them to bend or tear the cards.

At the end of the building process you can award prizes based on the following criteria:

1. Strength of the house
2. Number of levels
3. Difficulty
4. Creativity
5. Number of cards used
6. Teamwork
7. Tricks

Discussion: Depending on what you think will work best for your group choose one of the following discussion tracks:

1. To introduce the payment Christ made for us use: The Ultimate Credit Card
   or
2. If your kids are pretty familiar with what Christ did for us use: What Is Your Life Built On?

The Ultimate Credit Card

Open the discussion by asking how many different types of cards they can think of. Some answers:

Greeting cards; memory cards; playing cards; post cards; business cards; gas cards; gift cards; membership cards and, of course, credit cards.

<Show credit card commercial>

The credit card is an amazing thing. There are some, but very few, adults that do not have at least one credit card. Can someone tell me exactly how a credit card works? (You could get some pretty interesting answers here)

If you get a great explanation be sure to thank the kid that gave it. If you need to elaborate or explain further, be sure to give a simple to understand answer about how a credit card can be used to purchase items.

Most of them will already understand that concept–but what you want to focus on is the spending limit and that it needs to be paid on each month and if not paid in full there will be an interest charge on the amount carried to the next month.

Once all of that is explained and understood–to the best of their ability ask the following question:

Is it possible to be issued a credit card to pay off every debt you have, with no limit to how much you spend on it, and with no requirement to pay it back?

Hopefully you get no answers. If anyone says yes tell the kid that you have never heard of any credit card company that would issue such a card, but you would love the number of who to contact if he or she has a name. But they are right–there is one such guarantee of payment for all debts. It has no expiration date and you are not required to pay back the amount that you charge.

<Pull out your wallet and remove the cross-shaped credit card>

This credit card ensures that all my sins are paid for. It was issued to me when I accepted Jesus Christ into my heart and life. It has no expiration date and I can use it over and over. How it works is, if I do something that I know is a sin–like if I tell a lie, or if I have bad thoughts about someone that made me mad, or if I make a bad decision that goes against what God would want me to do, all I need to do is pray to God and tell Him I am sorry and ask Him to forgive me.

It's actually not a real credit card. It is a card that I made myself just to show you how easy it is to pay the price for your sins. The Bible tells us that every one of us is a sinner. There is only one person ever that never sinned and that was Jesus. That was His purpose–to be a perfect person with no sin. He then died on the cross to make that ultimate payment for our sins. If you believe that then you have your own credit card, just like this one–though you don't get an actual card. You get Jesus in your heart and He covers all of your sins–and since there is no way to pay Him back all that is required is for you to love Him for it and do the things with your life that would make Him happy.

This is a perfect opportunity to offer an invitation to accept Jesus. You need to be ready to offer one at anytime it is appropriate, and you need to be extremely comfortable with the words you use to share it. If you have not done so already prepare, in your own words, the words for your invitation. Remember, it needs to be simple for kids to understand, sincere in its tone and succinct in its delivery. For an example of an invitation you will find one in the "Salvation Invitation" section of this book.

If anyone accepts your invitation and asks Jesus into their heart for the first time please make it a special celebration with the rest of the group. It's not a time for embarrassment but they should be aware of their awesome step of faith. Tell them that there is a party in Heaven at that moment for the place that has been reserved for them!

What is Your Life Built On?

Open with a few questions:

How many of you were able to build your card house perfectly on the first try?

What happened if you weren't extremely careful?

<Show a clip of a house being built on top of a foundation>

Did you notice what the house was being built on? (Concrete slab or concrete walls)

FYI: Slabs, basements and crawl spaces are the three main foundation systems used on houses. In wet and coastal areas, it is sometimes common to put houses up on posts as well.

Do you know what that is called? (Foundation)

Do you know what it does? (The foundation transmits the weight from the building to the underlying ground.)

Do you know why a house needs a good foundation to build on? (Without a foundation the building has nothing to support it.)

A house is a lot like a person that way. A person needs many foundational things in their life for support.

What you learned when you were little—how to: walk; talk; get dressed; tie your shoes; everything you learned—was part of the foundation of learning.

What you are learning in school provides the foundation for your education. You learn things that you will use forever. For example–the Math skills you have learned will be used in so many things. How do you think you will use Math, even after you are done with school?

The most important thing in your life to act as a foundation is Jesus. Asking Jesus to come into your heart and your life is the strongest foundation you can have. When you do that you are asking Him to guide you as you make decisions on how to behave, to live, where to go in life. God has given us Jesus to be our foundation. Without the love of Jesus we would have no hope for a life in Heaven. He has also given us the Bible to teach us how to be more like Jesus. Finally, He has given us the Holy Spirit to be with us all the time and to be a guide for us in the things we do.

What would the world be like if Jesus had not come to save us from our sins? (You could get some pretty interesting answers here- cut it off if it begins to get out of hand)

What would your life be like without Jesus? (You could get some pretty interesting answers here)

If Jesus is not your foundation, do you want Him to be?

This is a perfect opportunity to offer an invitation to accept Jesus. You need to be ready to offer one at anytime it is appropriate, and you need to be extremely comfortable with the words you use to share it. If you have not done so already prepare, in your own words, the words for your invitation. Remember, it needs to be simple for kids to understand, sincere in its tone and succinct in its delivery. For an example of an invitation you will find one in the "Salvation Invitation" section of this book.

If anyone accepts your invitation and asks Jesus into their heart for the first time please make it a special celebration with the rest of the group. It's not a time for embarrassment but they should be aware of their awesome step of faith. Tell them that there is a party in Heaven at that moment for the place that has been reserved for them!

Closing Activity: Goliath Dodgeball or Doctor Dodgeball

This is basically good old dodgeball with the simple twist of each team has one player that is special. If "Dr. Dodgeball," then the specialty is that the player can "heal" a player that is out by touching them and they are then reinstated into the game. If you play "Goliath Dodgeball" the specialty is that, if hit, the entire team is immediately out and the opposing team wins the round.

The card he or she is holding determines the "special" player. You call out a number, and a suit if necessary based on the amount of cards given out. The kid on each team with that card is the designated special player. For added fun call out a different card for each team so they don't remember whom they were up against in prior games.

Supplies Needed for "Card" Based on Funds available

Activity	Budget	Budget w/ some frills	Bells & Whistles
General	-1 pack of cards to separate into teams -Pinneys		
Catch Me if You Can	-Masking tape for center line -Chairs -Stopwatch	Same	Same
Line Body Ball	-Giant Ball -Masking tape for goal lines -Cones	Same	Same
Line Soccer	-Kickball or soccer ball -Masking tape for goal lines -Cones	Same	Same
Card Houses	-1 pack of Playing cards per group	-Same plus additional packs of cards	Same
Discussion for "The Ultimate Credit Card" "What Is Your Life Built On?"	-Bible -TV & VCR -VHS recording of a credit card commercial -A homemade, cross-shaped credit card – it should fit in your wallet -A VHS recording of a house being built on concrete foundation – there are many television shows you can record this from.		
Goliath or Dr. Dodgeball	-Balls that don't hurt when hit by them	Same	Same

Change

Theme Target:

Teach kids about how we are changed when we invite Jesus into our lives.

Golden Nugget:

Jesus completely changes your life; beginning at the moment He enters it and continuing until the end of it.

Scripture:

Acts 9:1–19 (The Message)

Separate the kids into two teams. Give one team pinneys to wear.

Activity #1: Change-Up Soccer

This is soccer, with a major change—you cannot use your feet.

Make a large grid on the floor, using masking tape. Plan plenty of time to accomplish this. If you have a "Tape Layer" this will be a tremendous blessing!

There should be enough boxes in the grid for each player to have their own box. The goals should be beyond the grid, with a box in front of it for the goalie. Use two cones for each goal.

Put a piece of colored tape in each box—you need two different colors, one for each team. Pinneys are one color of tape, non-pinneys another.

It should look like this:

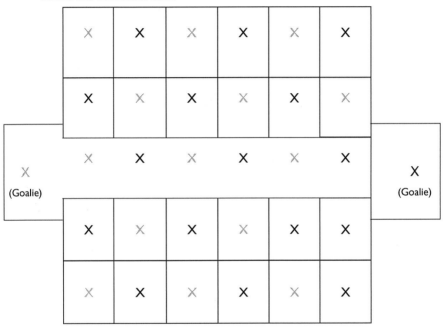

Each team is attempting to score goals. A goal is scored when the ball goes through the cones, at a height that can be defended–use your own judgment as to whether a goal was too high.

Players must each be in their own square and they must be in a square marked with their color of tape. It's okay to have empty squares. The four corners would be the best place to start emptying and then on to the center. Remove the tape from those boxes so they remain empty permanently.

Any time you blow the whistle and yell "Change squares" each player, including the goalie, must move to a new box marked with their color. They cannot return to a box they previously occupied.

For added fun, once they have the hang of it, play with more than one ball. Also, to add to your theme use a ball that changes color from body heat. "Gertie" makes a ball that fits this description, and it is a safe playing ball.

Rules of play:

1. No "field" player may use his or her feet. Goalies may use any part of their body to block a goal.

2. No "field" player may throw the ball. They can only move the ball out of their square by hitting it with a part of their body other than their feet. Goalies may throw the ball–but cannot score.

3. No player may step over the line of their square–they can reach over to try to steal the ball from their opponent, but cannot step over.

4. A player may catch the ball but may not hold on to it. Ball must be in constant motion.

5. Ball may be hit volleyball style but no spiking at a player, except at the goalie.

6. Ball can be stolen from the hands of opposing player but not by hitting or pushing them. Think Basketball foul at that point.

Activity #2: Change-Up Tag (elbow tag)

Instruct kids to get a partner but a pinney cannot partner with another pinney—so that all partners are a pinney/non-pinney duo. Have partners link elbows and stand anywhere in the playing area, leaving at least ten feet between each pair. Choose one pair to start it off. One is it and trying to catch the other. If the chaser tags the runner they immediately swap roles and the original runner has to tag him back. A runner can escape being tagged (and take a rest from running) by simply running to one of the standing pairs and linking elbows with one of the pair to make a threesome.

In this game, two is company but three is a crowd! When the runner latches on, the one member of the pair whose arm was not linked with must break away at top speed. This player instantly becomes new prey for "It"—until he dashes to yet another pair for safety. The confusing transitions can provide a break for weary runners and give even a slow moving "It" a chance to catch the runner.

Always be ready to change it up yourself when "It" is struggling or if some kids aren't getting a turn to run.

Activity #3: Hockey Wiffle Ball

Play like Wiffle ball but the bat is a hockey stick and the ball is rolled or bounced as the pitch. Use different style balls based on ability or just to change it up. Example: A strong kid should get a spongy type ball that won't travel as far and fast as another type. A weaker player should get a ball like the "Gertie" ball that will travel farther with less force.

To allow everyone equal opportunities to play don't bother with the number of outs or strikes. Bat through the entire team each inning and only count the runs that scored. If they get out, fine, they are out and didn't score, but let everyone bat before switching offense and defense.

Discussion: How does Jesus change your life?

<Keep some silly putty that changes color with heat close to you during the discussion. It needs to be kept cool though so consider having a mug that is full of ice water next to you during the discussion—one that the kids can't see has ice in it. Flatten the silly putty and put it along the side of the mug that the kids can't see.>

Open by watching a classic episode of The Brady Bunch. It is available on DVD or, if you check local listings ahead of time you may be able to record it off of your TV. Anyway, it is from Season three and the episode title is "Dough Re Mi." This is the one where the Brady kids singing group is affected by the fact that Peter's voice is changing. It includes the song "When It's Time to Change."

Peter was growing up. When boys begin to mature their voices change and become deeper. At the point that the change is taking place it can be awkward since it doesn't happen overnight. So, just like with Peter, their voices can crack here and there, rather unexpectedly.

Lots of changes take place as you grow up. You get taller; voice changes; you get wiser; and you get to do lots of things that you have been looking forward to doing for a long time–like driving; finishing school; earning money and gaining independence.

Change happens all the time. Sometimes the changes are GREAT and sometimes not so great. Have any of you had something change in your life recently?

There are lots of stories in the Bible about change. There is one in particular about somebody that went through a major change. His name was Saul.

Saul was alive at the same time Jesus was going around and teaching people about God and the kingdom in Heaven. Jesus was telling people that He was God's Son and that following Him would allow them to enter into Heaven when they were finished with their lives on earth. Many people believed Him, but in order to do so they had to believe that He was who He said He was. That was hard for a lot of people because it meant that they had to change what they were taught.

Before God sent Jesus people were taught that they must obey God's laws and offer sacrifices of animals to be protected from His wrath when they sinned. Jesus taught that God loved them and that He was sent to provide a new way to enter into Heaven. That meant that they didn't have to do things as strictly as before and that they no longer had to sacrifice animals to have their sins forgiven. Jesus was going to die for them instead and that His death would cover every sin from then on.

Saul grew up Jewish, meaning He had been taught the ways that Jesus was saying were not necessary anymore. Jesus said that people needed to love God and love others and do what was right according to that. That was a big change from what Saul believed. He also thought that Jesus was a liar and that there was no way He could be God's Son.

Saul was determined to not allow Jesus' teachings to be accepted. He began putting Jesus' followers into jail and treating them very badly. He thought they were just plain wrong and he would not allow it.

The story goes like this:

Saul was breathing down the necks of the Master's disciples, out for the kill. He went to the Chief Priest and got arrest warrants to take to the meeting places in Damascus so that if he found anyone there that was following Jesus, whether men or women, he could arrest them and bring them to Jerusalem.

He set off. When he got to the outskirts of Damascus, he was suddenly dazed by a blinding flash of light. As he fell to the ground, he heard a voice: "Saul, Saul, why are you out to get me?"

He said, "Who are you, Master?"

"I am Jesus, the One you're hunting down. I want you to get up and enter the city. In the city you'll be told what to do next."

His companions stood there dumbstruck—they could hear the sound, but couldn't see anyone—while Saul, picking himself up off the ground, found himself stone-blind. They had to take him by the hand and lead him into Damascus. He continued blind for three days.

There was a disciple in Damascus by the name of Ananias. The Master spoke to him in a vision: "Ananias."

"Yes, Master?" he answered.

"Get up and go over to Straight Avenue. Ask at the house of Judas for a man from Tarsus. His name is Saul. He's there praying. He has just had a dream in which he saw a man named Ananias enter the house and lay hands on him so he could see again."

Ananias protested, "Master, you can't be serious. Everybody's talking about this man and the terrible things he's been doing, his reign of terror against your people in Jerusalem! And now he's shown up here with papers from the Chief Priest that give him license to do the same to us."

But the Master said, "Don't argue. Go! I have picked him as my personal representative to non-Jews and kings and Jews. And now I'm about to show him what he's in for—the hard suffering that goes with this job."

So Ananias went and found the house, placed his hands on blind Saul, and said, "Brother Saul, the Master sent me, the same Jesus you saw on your way here. He sent me so you could see again and be filled with the Holy Spirit."

No sooner were the words out of his mouth something like scales fell from Saul's eyes—he could see again! He got to his feet, was baptized, and sat down with them to a hearty meal.

Saul changed immediately. From that moment on, instead of trying to put Christians in jail he began teaching new people about Jesus. He spent the rest of His life teaching that Jesus was who He said He was and that believing in Him and following Him was the only way to enter into the Kingdom of God.

He also changed his name from Saul to Paul. Everyone knew that Saul was against Jesus and the new believers so he used the name Paul so that people would listen to him.

<Pull out your silly putty and hold it up for everyone to see>

Imagine this bit of silly putty is your life. <Holding on to just a small portion of it show it around so each kid sees it. Close your hand over the silly putty and begin kneading it.>

<Slowly state, as you squeeze the putty in your hands being careful to not let it be seen>

You are flexible… and moldable… and when you place your life in the hands of Jesus something amazing happens… He begins shaping you to be the person He wants you to be and… He changes you immediately.

<Hold up the silly putty for all the kids to see>

See how it has changed?

If you choose to do so this is a perfect opportunity to offer an invitation to accept Jesus. You need to be ready to offer one at anytime it is appropriate, and you need to be extremely comfortable with the words you use to share it. If you have not done so already prepare, in your own words, the words for your invitation. Remember, it needs to be simple for kids to understand, sincere in its tone and succinct in its delivery. For an example of an invitation you will find one in the "Salvation Invitation" section of this book.

If anyone accepts your invitation and asks Jesus into their heart for the first time please make it a special celebration with the rest of the group. It's not a time for embarrassment but they should be aware of their awesome step of faith. Tell them that there is a party in Heaven at that moment for the place that has been reserved for them!

Closing Activity: Change-Up Dodgeball

This is likely to be everyone's favorite version of dodgeball once you play it.

In this version everyone is on his or her own team and can run anywhere. There is only one ball–preferably a really large ball, approximately 36." Bigens is a brand name for a large ball like this. It's a great addition to your supply closet too–for "Giant night," or to play this game as often as you need a filler activity for your kids.

How to play:

1. Just like regular dodgeball, you are out if you get hit with the ball directly. If it touches the ground first you are not out.

2. You are also out if you throw the ball at a player and they catch it. This is no easy task with this size ball—so it adds a degree of difficulty for the kids that normally get everyone out by catching a throw. They take more of a risk by trying to catch the ball.

3. The player that has the ball may only take one step with it–eliminating the dominant player that chases everyone down and gets him or her out. If they take more than one step with the ball they are out. There are ways to move with the ball that don't require holding on to it: Dribbling and rolling. The fun is that they are at risk of losing it since they must pick it up and throw it to get someone out. Steals are fun for the kids!!

4. When a player gets out they still need to pay attention to the game because when the players that got them out get out themselves they can return to the game—unlimited redemption! So

the game is always changing and they don't have to wait for an ultimate winner to re-enter the game.

5. Players that get out by taking more than one step can re-enter if another kid gets out by doing the same thing or by allowance from the game leader. Don't make them sit out longer than normal, but do insist they sit out for breaking the rule.

★   By the way–this is a GREAT game for leaders to play too!!

Supplies Needed for this Event Based on Funds available			
Activity	Budget	Budget w/ some frills	Bells & Whistles
Change-Up Soccer	-Lots of rolls of masking tape for the grid -2 different colors of masking tape for the X's in each box -4 cones -Pinneys -Safe ball – consider a ball that changes from body heat – like a "Gertie" Ball	Same	Same
Change-Up Tag	Nothing	Same	Same
Hockey Wiffle Ball	-4 Bases -1 hockey stick -Lots of different size and type of balls.	Same	Same
Discussion	-TV/VCR or DVD Player -Brady Bunch "Dough Re Mi" episode from season 3. This is the one where Peter's voices is changing and it affects the Brady singing group. Show the whole episode – 22 minutes long. -Color - Changing Silly Putty -Cup or mug of ice water	Same	Same
Change-Up Dodgeball	-Big Ball (36" Bigens ball is a great addition to your supply closet)	Same	Same

Choices...

Theme Target:

Teach kids about Free Will, the consequences of choices, and how to choose life over death.

Golden Nugget:

Choose Life!

Scripture:

John 3:16 (NIV)

For this event you will actually need to have two separate activities planned in each activity slot. You will give the kids the choice between two items or ideas, without giving away either activity. Without knowing what they are getting into they must choose which activity they are going to participate in and go to the designated area for it. Once they have made their choice you present the activity. They cannot change their minds though after they have finalized their choice.

Each activity will also have prizes. They will choose their prize, without knowing what it is. The prizes will be in bags or containers that they can't see through. They choose based on the outside appearance. Again, make them stick with their choice.

If you typically provide a snack during your event carry the theme through in this area as well. Offer two choices of snack–they must choose up front though. Perhaps they choose fork or spoon and each snack requires one of them. The snacks should both be good though, not like some of the prizes.

Some choices will be Awesome and some... not so great. You will have some disappointed kids, but this is an amazing learning tool. Be prepared for some tears, but hold your ground.

Activity #1: Would you rather Catch or Dodge?

Catching choice: **Cheez Head**

Separate the kids into two teams. Place two chairs in the center, side-by-side, and facing opposite directions. Place a line of masking tape at either end of the "court" that the kids cannot step over.

Each team elects one person to represent them. You can choose whether they know what they are getting into or not–it's fun for the leaders when they don't know. The chosen kid sits in the middle and you cover his or her head in plastic–either a shower cap or Saran Wrap Covers (medium size).

Next, cover the plastic on their heads in shaving cream. To prevent getting any in eyes you could provide glasses or goggles. On "GO" each team throws cheese balls at their teammate to see which team can catch the most cheese balls. They can only throw one cheese ball at a time. They cannot step over the line on a throw. The kid in the center can lean to catch the cheese ball but can't leave the chair. Either play in specified time or until cheese balls are gone. The team whose kid has the most cheese balls on his head at the end wins the game.

Leader alerts leader of alternate activity that clean up is about to begin so they know how long they have to play. Everyone helps clean up and then move on to next activity.

Dodging choice: **Dodge the Rolling Balls**

First, separate the kids into small groups of two or three kids, depending on how many chose this activity. Next make one big circle or square with all the people, and send one of the groups in the middle. The surrounding groups sit down while the group in the middle stands up. Now the surrounding groups will roll all the dodge balls towards the group in the middle, which will try to dodge all the balls coming at them in every direction. Once they get hit they are out. The last person standing is the winner.

After you have Group one go, have Group two take a turn, and so on. At the very end have all the winners come up to determine the super, ultra, mega winner.

Before moving on to the next activity all winners, in either choice, choose a prize.

Bring out two paper bags–be creative and make the bags look different: one appealing, one not. Kids choose which bag their prize will come from and then they get one of whatever is in the bag. Make them stick with their choice. Be prepared for disappointment but remember… it's all part of the teaching opportunity.

Activity 2: Would you rather shoot or swat?

Shooting choice: **Marshmallow shooters**

Break up into two teams. One team on either side of court (square marked off with masking tape, or if room is small then both teams line up against opposing walls. Put two buckets or containers in center of two teams and give each player a Marshmallow shooter (three to four inch length of ¾ inch clear tube). Each player then gets five mini marshmallows. Each team is shooting for their bucket in the center. Each player shoots one marshmallow at a time. Team with most marshmallows in the bucket at the end wins the game.

★ Tip: This works best to put the marshmallow in the tube so it is not hanging out at all, and then blow through the other end. Marshmallows will get moist and leave sticky residue if they put it in their mouth and then shoot through entire tube.

Note: Shooters are reusable after thorough washing.

Swatting choice: **Flyswatter Hockey**

This is hockey with flyswatters as the sticks. Use a small ball–plastic golf ball or ping-pong ball. Note: If using ping-pong ball have extras on hand. If stepped on they will no longer be worthwhile for game.

Before moving on to next activity all winners, in either choice, choose a prize.

Activity #3: Would you rather sit still or be wiggly?

Sit still choice: **Mumball**

Each player gets a folding chair. They place their chair randomly in a designated area, attempting to face all other players. Each player sits on the chair with their buttocks on the top of the chair back and their feet on the seat.

The referee hands a ball to one player who starts the game. The player throws the ball to any other player, making sure the ball is catchable. A ball is not catchable if the player would have needed to leave their sitting position to catch the ball. A player that lifts his buttocks off the chair to catch a ball is out unless the throw caused it. If the ball is caught play continues with the current ball holder. If the ball is missed a player must sit down on their seat. The player that sits is the one that was at fault for the miss: if catchable, the catcher sits; if not catchable the thrower sits. One other thing for this game—the players are not allowed to make any noise–hence, the Mum part. Any player that makes any noise not required for normal bodily functions is out and must sit. Last player left is the winner and starts the next round.

Wiggly choice: **Hula wiggle**

Separate the kids into two teams, if there are enough kids who chose to be wiggly. Have all participants in each team form a circle holding each other's hands. Get someone to 'unlock' one of his or her hands from the circle, put a hula-hoop onto his/her hand, and then reconnect with the circle.

The aim of this game is to get the hula-hoop around the circle and back to where it started without the group letting go of each other's hands.

Before moving on to next activity all winners, in either choice, choose a prize.

Activity #4: Would you rather eat or sit?

Eating choice: **Musical Food**

Players stand in a circle and pass a bag around from one player to the next while music plays. The bag has various food items in it. When the music stops the player left holding the bag pulls out one item and eats it.

Suggested items in bag: Spam cubes individually wrapped in saran wrap; small wrapped candy; cooked, plain macaroni; bites of cereal; bite-sized vegetables; lemon wedge

You can either have all items in one bag and they reach in and take out one piece or a different bag for each round, or they can pass around a different object and when they have to choose they can choose which bag they pull their item from.

Use lively music, preferably something that has food as its subject. One suggestion would be John Lithgow's "Everybody Eats When they Come to My House," from his children's CD entitled "Singin' in the Bathtub"

Sitting choice: **Seat of your pants Nuke 'Em**

Separate the kids into two teams. Set up a makeshift volleyball net, lower than normal–a rope tied or duct taped to two chairs would suffice here. If you have nothing you could always have leaders on their knees with their arms outstretched to serve as the net–this is very tiring for the leaders but fun for you and the kids to watch.

Players sit on the floor and play Nuke 'Em over the "net"

Before moving on to the Discussion all winners, in either choice, choose a prize.

Discussion: Free Will–Would you rather live or die?

Watch a clip from Disney's Aladdin–the part when the Genie is explaining the rules of wishes to Aladdin. You will capitalize on the point he makes about not being able to make someone fall in love with another person.

If you prefer you could show a clip from Bruce Almighty—the part where God is explaining to Bruce that people have free will.

So, what is important about what the genie said about making a person fall in love with him? or What is important about what God told Bruce about not making his girlfriend love him?

Everyone has the right to choose who they love, right?

What if someone you don't really like or know very well loves you very, very much. Does that mean that you are required to love them too?

Your parents might say that you have to love them but we all know that sometimes we just pretend to love some people to their face, but we don't really want to.

That is called "Free Will." We each have the right to choose how we feel about things or people. We also have the right to choose how we behave. Again, you have to obey your parents but inside your heart, where it really matters, they can't decide how you really feel. You get to choose that for yourself.

That's the same way it is with God. He loves you more than anyone else ever could and He wants nothing more than for you to choose to love and follow Him, but He won't make that choice for you. God gave every single one of us the right and responsibility to choose that for ourselves.

What does that mean?

-See what the kids think that means.

It means yes; God loves each and every one of us very much. The Bible tells us that He loves us so much that He gave us a way to defeat Satan and the sin that he offers. The Bible also tells us that every one of us has that sin in our lives and that there is only one way to pay for that sin, which is death.

No, that doesn't mean that if you disobey your Mom and go to a friend's house without cleaning up your room that you will die on your way home because of it. What it means is that there is true life and death for your soul—the part of you that makes you who you are, not just your body. Every one of our bodies will die—that's just part of life—our bodies are not made to live forever. But our bodies are not our souls, or the heart of who we are.

As humans we sin. That's the way it is. Satan takes great pleasure in that fact. What Satan doesn't enjoy is that God loves us so much that He gave us a way to pay for our sin—so that we don't have to pay for it ourselves. God gave us Jesus. He paid for our sin by dying on the cross. That is what He came for. He never sinned and that is what made Him the perfect one to pay for us. He was God's Son and He died so that we don't have to.

So, the way to pay is there for us. But we still have to actually choose it. If we want to make Satan happy and don't choose Jesus then we are choosing to die and then be in hell with Satan. He likes that because it is one less person that chooses to live in Heaven with God. If we choose Jesus then we choose to live. We choose to have our sin paid for by Him and to go to Heaven when our bodies die.

But we still have to choose. Nobody can choose this for you—not me, or your friends, or even your parents. You have the right and responsibility to choose this for yourself.

Just like in all the games we played earlier, and then the prizes—you have to choose what you are going to do. With those things you didn't know what you were choosing. Would it be the game you really wanted to play? Would it be the better of the two prizes? You didn't know until you chose it.

In this case you know what you are choosing before you choose it. If you choose Jesus you are choosing life. He will come into your heart and take away your sin. Just to let you know though, there is responsibility in choosing Jesus. You are also choosing to try to make good choices for the rest of your life too. To live in a way that will be pleasing to God—the One who loves you and gave you this choice to begin with. If you choose not to accept Jesus you are choosing not to live in a way that pleases God.

So, if you haven't already chosen Jesus in the past you have a choice to make now. Do you want to choose to have Him come into your heart and take away your sins? Do you want to choose life? If you do I want to tell you how to do that. It is very simple and only takes a moment, but it is the most important moment of your life. (See "Salvation Invitation" for an example of how to lead them in inviting Christ into their life.)

At this point you have offered the invitation and you can lead them in prayer. You need to be comfortable with the prayer and use words that are simple and they will understand. If you have not done so already prepare, in your own words, the words for your invitation. Remember, it needs to be simple for kids to understand, sincere in its tone and succinct in its delivery. For an example of an invitation you will find one in the "Salvation Invitation" section of this book.

If anyone accepts your invitation and asks Jesus into their heart for the first time please make it a special celebration with the rest of the group. It's not a time for embarrassment but they should be aware of their awesome step of faith. Tell them that there is a party in Heaven at that moment for the place that has been reserved for them!

Closing Activity: Would you rather give or take?

Give choice: **Hamper Ball**

Separate your group into two teams. Hamper ball is basketball, but the goals are hampers or clean trashcans. Play just like basketball. Fouls turn ball over to other team. Use discretion on flagrant fouls and offer penalty shots–free shot from specific location. Goalie or no goalie is up to you. If there's a goalie be sure to switch them out after every goal. If there is no goalie then tape off a section and put the hamper in the center. Players cannot enter the taped off section to shoot.

Take Choice: **Steal the Earth**

Steal the bacon with a giant ball. If you don't have a giant ball then use any ball—giant is just really fun to watch. Separate your group into two teams. Within the teams, starting with the smallest kid, assign each player on each team a number, one through the highest number of players on the largest team. If teams are uneven choose kids to be multiple numbers and then be careful not to call those numbers together—unless team is losing really bad and needs an advantage. Yes, you have the right to do that!

Place the ball in the center of the two teams. When you call a number the players with that number run out and try to get the ball back to their team. If it's a giant ball no additional rules are necessary. If it's a small ball: if they are touched by the opposing player while holding the ball they must drop it where they are and go back to their team and be tagged by a player before they can go back for the ball. There are ways around this if they figure it out–they can roll the ball, or kick the ball, or even dribble the ball. You decide though whether the ball must be carried over their line to count as a score.

A variation of this game is to get the ball across the other team's line instead of taking it to their own. The line is then involved in preventing the ball from crossing the line. You would need a line for each team to defend.

Before closing give every kid a choice of prize–this time though, both bags have the same prize and both are good.

Supplies Needed for "Choices" Based on Funds available			
Activity	Budget	Budget w/ some frills	Bells & Whistles
Cheez Head	-Plastic tarp or drop cloth -2 chairs -2 shower caps or Saran wrap covers -2 cans shaving cream -2 containers cheese balls	Same	Same
Dodge the Rolling Balls	-Balls (soft ones that don't hurt when hit)	Same	Same
Marshmallow shooters	-Plastic tarp or drop cloth – a sheet also works -Marshmallow shooters made from clear plastic tubing (any hardware store carries this) with diameter large enough for mini marshmallow – ¾". Cut tubing into 3-4" lengths - 2 containers of mini marshmallows -2 buckets or containers to shoot at – cake pans work nice and allow for bounces both in or out -Masking tape if needed to keep lines at appropriate distance	Same	Same

Flyswatter Hockey	-Cheap wire flyswatters – enough for each player -Ping-pong or small plastic ball -Laundry baskets for goals -Masking tape or cones for boundaries	Same but with small street hockey or soccer goals	Same
Mumball	-Folding chairs or stationary chairs -Ball -Cones to designate area	Same	Same
Hula Wiggle	2 Hula-hoops	Same	Same
Musical Food	-CD player -CD w/ lively music -Paper bags with food items -Food items: Bite-sized candy, veggies, fruit, etc. Some tasty, some not – Be creative	Same	Same
Seat of Your Pants Nuke Em	-Cones or masking tape for boundaries -2 chairs -Rope -Duct tape -Ball	-Same but with Pennant flag rope for the net	Same but with lowered volleyball or badminton net
Discussion	-Bible -TV -VCR or DVD player -Aladdin or Bruce Almighty video or DVD	Same	Same
Hamper Ball	-2 hampers or clean trash cans -Ball -Cones or masking tape for boundaries	Same	Same
Steal the Earth	-Cones or masking tape for boundaries -Ball	Same but use a Giant ball	Same

Dare

Theme Target:

Teach the kids what following Jesus means.

Golden Nugget:

Daniel dared to stand up for what he believed. "I dare you to do be like Daniel!"

Scripture:

Daniel 6 (The Message)

This event is lengthy and it could easily be a full day event. Pick and choose what you like best to pare it down or spread it all out over two separate sessions if your event doesn't dictate a full day's worth of activities. Kids should be forewarned to wear old clothes and sneakers and to bring a change of clothes for their ride home.

Separate into two or more teams, depending on your supplies. Keep the teams the same for the entire event and keep track of the score throughout the entire event. Each activity is a "dare" and points will be awarded based on level of completion–not every kid will complete the dare, some won't even be willing to try some of them. By that description you should know that you and your leaders are probably going to enjoy watching these activities as much as they will enjoy participating in them.

Remember, it is amazing what kids will do–even for just a few points. Be prepared to end a kids' participation if it will cause them undue hardship–for example: The Baby Bottle Chug could leave some kids feeling queasy. All leaders should be instructed to release a kid from completing the activity in the name of healthy bellies.

Provide each kid with his own washcloth before the first activity. Instruct them that they only get one for the day and they will need it, and that you want each one back at the end of the day/evening. They will lose big points from their team's score if they don't return it. You don't need to remove points at the end–most kids that may lose it will feel bad enough as it is. This will cause them to be more cautious with it though.

You will need a competent scorekeeper for the entire event–though, the points don't need to be 100% accurate since the kids will never be able to keep track of it. Periodically the points should be announced. The closer the points stay the more exciting it will be for the kids to participate so **Scorekeepers Allowance should be invoked.** (See the chapter entitled "Housekeeping For Your Ministry")

Points should be awarded to each player according to level of completion:

1. Accepts the dare and satisfactorily completes it: twenty points

2. Accepts the dare, attempts it but does not complete it: ten points

3. Refuses the dare completely: 0 points

4. The team that completes the challenge first and is sitting quietly: twenty-five points

5. Bonus points are awarded to the team that has the most players accept the dare: five points per player.

6. Begin the explanation of each game with the following: "I dare you to . . ." Explain the challenge and then ask: "Do you accept this dare?"

Activity #1: Pin the Tail

This is an "up-front game" and it's really just to humor you and the other leaders... and to get the ball rolling, but the kids don't have to know that.

Tell them: *"I dare you to pin a tail?"*

Pin the tail on the donkey–or whatever you want to pin something on. *"Do you accept this dare? Who wants to go first?"*

Select the kid or several kids if you have enough supplies to run more than one at a time, which will be the best sport(s) about the joke.

Now for the fun part: Pull out the donkey(s) and have a leader hold it (them). Now "look" for the tails (that you really don't have). Make a big deal about forgetting to pack the tails in your stuff, but don't go overboard with it. Pull out a marker.

"OK, since I forgot the tails I guess we'll just do this with our fingers and a marker. We'll blindfold you and spin you around. Then, you press your finger to where you would have pinned the tail and I'll mark the spot with this marker. Then, the closest mark wins the game."

Go through the motions as noted above. While they are spinning silently instruct the rest of the kids to be quiet and don't give away the joke.

"Okay, now, you're facing the donkey. Go ahead and decide where to place your finger."

At this point, the leaders holding the donkeys lower them and reveal a container filled with peanut butter (be careful of allergies though) or mashed black beans. The leader holds the container up so that when they press their finger against the "donkey" they actually put their finger into the stuff.

The kids get a big kick out of it.

Activity #2: Dirty Diaper Relay

"I dare you to eat some yummy pudding."

On "GO" one kid at a time runs (or rides a scooter, or skateboards—you decide the degree of the challenge) down to a table that has a "dirty diaper" waiting for them. The dirt is pudding that has been put into a clean diaper. The kid must eat all the pudding out of the diaper, without using his hands. When the leader supervising the table is satisfied with their completion they head back to their line and tag the next victim… er player.

The first team to get all players to complete it and is sitting quietly, wins the game.

"Do you accept this dare?"

Activity #3: Chee-toes (another relay)

"I dare you to feed a partner."

Within their team the kids that accept the dare need to get a part-ner–if uneven one kid needs to go twice. On "Go" the pair runs down to a chair. One of them sits on the chair and takes their shoe and sock off of one foot. The other kid lies down on the floor next to the chair. A leader puts three cheetoes on the floor next to them. The barefoot kid must pick up one cheeto at a time and "feed" it to their partner. Once all three chee-toes are eaten the two run back to their line and tag the next player. The first team to complete the challenge, has all members sitting quietly with their shoes back on their feet and tied properly, wins the bonus points.

Though this is obviously unsanitary to begin with the cheetoes could be placed on a napkin on the floor and not directly on the floor itself. Doesn't make it much cleaner but–that's the whole point of the dare.

Do you accept this dare?"

Activity #4: Spamalot Relay

"I dare you to "bob" for a yummy treat."

One at a time the kids run down to the tub of water with spam cubes in it. They must put their head in and eat one spam cube to complete this challenge. Once eaten, they go back to their team and tag the next player. Instruct them that the treat in the tub is a surprise and they are not allowed to say anything about what they have eaten. They will lose points for their team if they say anything about it.

The first team to get all players to complete it and is sitting quietly, wins the game.

"Do you accept this dare?"

Activity #5: Jello Slurp and Spit Relay

"I dare you to slurp jello."

One at a time each kid runs down to the table and slurps as much jello as they can into their straw. They run back and spit it into their team's cup. Each team's cup has a mark on it. The first team to fill their cup to the mark and have all members sitting quietly wins the bonus points.

Note: Straws with the greatest diameter speeds up this game and definitely not the bendable type. Also, depending on the stiffness of the jello it is surprisingly difficult to slurp it into the straw and then get it back out. Some kids will figure out that if they shoot saliva through the straw with the jello that it will increase their deposit–and really, who is going to check the balance of jello to saliva?

If they figure out a good strategy encourage them to share it with the rest of their team.

"Do you accept this dare?"

Activity #6: Balloon Bottom Squash Relay–do this outdoors

"I dare you to pop a balloon."

Ahead of time fill enough balloons for one per kid with shaving cream. This is not as easy as it sounds–allow plenty of time and get plenty of helpers.

One at a time the kids will run down and be handed a balloon. They must put the balloon on the ground and sit on it to pop it. Once the balloon is popped they return to their team and tag the next player.

The first team to get all players to complete it and is sitting quietly, wins the game.

"Do you accept this dare?"

Activity #7: Wormalot

"I dare you to eat a worm."

This is the same as "Spamalot" but they bob for gummy worms instead. This is so fun to watch since those things are slippery little guys. For an additional degree of nastiness use the water from Spamalot. Keep the water shallow since gummy worms sink to the bottom.

The first team to get all of the players to complete it and is sitting quietly, wins the game.

"Do you accept this dare?"

Activity #8: Olive You

"I dare you to spit an olive."

Give each team a jar of olives. One at a time each kid will take one olive and put it in their mouth. They walk to a designated line (they cannot cross the line). They then spit their olive, attempting to land it in a cake pan (or other goal). The olive must stay in the pan to count. They continue until all the olives from their jar are gone.

For an added challenge put the pans close together. If they score for the other team it counts for the other team.

The team with the most olives in their pan and has all members sitting quietly wins the game.

"Do you accept this dare?"

Activity #9: Juicy Juice–outside activity

"I dare you to get juicy."

Put a bunch of grapes or peeled oranges into a tub for each team. Each player must remove his or her shoes and socks. On "Go" the kids have a good old-fashioned grape (or orange) stomping. In pairs of two they will each stomp for one or two minutes—you decide that. Play some fun music during this time.

They will think that the dare is to stomp the fruit but really, the dare is to dip a Dixie cup into the pool and have a drink of the juice that is produced.

"Do you accept this dare?"

You will actually have a few freakish kids that will do this. Be prepared for fallout from the parents.

Activity #10: Baby Bottle Chug

"I dare you to act like a baby."

One at a time each kid will run down to the table and pick up a baby bottle (use the smallest ones you can get and put one or two ounces of prune juice in each). They then chug the contents of the bottle as quickly as possible. Cut a slit into the nipple of each bottle to speed this race up. Once done, they return to their team and tag the next player.

The first team to get all players to complete it and is sitting quietly, wins the game.

"Do you accept this dare?"

Activity #11: Ketchup With Me

"I dare you to eat some M & M's"

One at a time each player runs down to the table, takes a spoonful of ketchup covered M & M's. They must eat the whole thing and then run back to their team and tag the next player.

The first team to get all players to complete it and is sitting quietly, wins the game.

"Do you accept this dare?"

Activity #12: Snoot Shoot

"I dare you to shoot a skittle."

Same as Olive You but each team gets a pack of skittles.

Each kid puts a skittle in one nostril, covers the other nostril and then shoots it into the cake pan.

The first team to get all players to complete it and is sitting quietly, wins the game.

"Do you accept this dare?"

Activity #13: Stinky Soda Swig

"I dare you to drink some soda."

This one could be pretty nasty if it has been rainy or the kids have been shoeless so think twice before doing it, especially if it is at the end of the day.

Have the kids remove one shoe and sock. Give each one a cup or small can of soda. Instruct them to put their sock over the cup or can. On "Go" they are to drink the soda through their sock. If you want to do this one but be nicer you could bring a bunch of old but clean socks–just so they look old and possibly dirty–and use them. For an added touch bring them in a laundry bag.

The first team to get all players to complete it and is sitting quietly, wins the game. It's a good idea to have a baggie to put their sock in to take it home.

Activity #14: Don't Forget to Brush

"I dare you to fight cavities."

The kids must partner up with a teammate. They then decide which one will squirt and which one will catch.

The catcher lies on his back on a disposable plastic dropcloth or trash bag. He holds a Dixie cup that has a mark at ½ way on it, over his belly.

The squirter stands over him, but facing him. Blindfold the squirter.

On "Go" the squirter begins squirting and the catcher tries to catch all the toothpaste being squirted in the Dixie cup. The catcher needs to give directions to the squirter to help him–like, "Slow down, Speed Up, etc." The first team that has a pair fill to the line wins the bonus points.

Activity #14: Stinky Twinkies (or cupcakes, or whatever)

"I dare you to eat a Twinkie."

On "Go" each player eats a twinkie as quickly as possible. You can either be nice and use this as your snack or have a little fun with it by slicing the twinkie or cupcake open, replacing the filling with something unexpected–rice krispies, a cucumber slice–you decide whether it's a good surprise or bad.

The first team to get all players to complete it and is sitting quietly, wins the game.

"Do you accept this dare?"

Activity #17: Steal the Bacon

"I dare you to steal the bacon."

Play "steal the bacon"–with actual bacon. Put a disposable plastic dropcloth in the center of the playing field. Instruct players to take their shoes and socks off. Squirt watered down ketchup or BBQ sauce or something like that all over the tarp to make it slippery and gross–or just use soapy water–you decide the degree of messiness on this one.

Within the teams, starting with the smallest kid, assign each player on each team a number, one through the highest number of players on the largest team. If teams are uneven one kid gets a second number and you don't call those numbers at the same time unless you want to give the other team an advantage.

When their number is called they race out to steal the bacon and get it back across their team's line first. If tagged while holding the bacon they must drop it and return to their team to be tagged by a player on the line before they can go for the bacon again. They can toss the bacon toward their line but it must be carried across the line to score.

The team with the most scores after every kid has participated, or until you are ready to be done with this game, wins the game.

Discussion #1 (fit in schedule wherever you prefer): Daniel in the Lion's Den

Show a clip of a lion tamer—you could find this on a circus DVD or video–if you would like.

It takes many years of practice and dedication to tame a lion. Do any of you have interest in learning how to work with lions like that guy?

Do you know that, a long time ago, some people used lions as a punishment or weapon?

There is a story in the Bible about some guys that did exactly that.

Daniel was a good man and He loved God. Daniel knew God's laws and he refused to follow any law that was against God's law.

The king really liked Daniel. He had appointed him to a very high position in the kingdom. He trusted him and looked to him for advice.

But Daniel had a problem. There were some guys that worked for the king that didn't like Daniel. They were jealous of him because the king favored him over them.

They decided to get rid of Daniel and they knew just how to do it. They used the king's pride. Every king is proud and wants to be given praise and honor. The king was good but he still liked being king and all of the perks that come with it.

So these men got the king to issue a law that all of the people of the king-

dom would have to pray to and worship the King and nobody else. These men knew that Daniel would never do it. They also told the king that there should be a harsh punishment for disobeying the law. They told him that anyone that broke this law should be killed by being thrown into a lion's den. The king liked that he would be the center of everyone's attention so he agreed to the law.

Daniel knew that it was wrong to obey the new law. God had commanded that only God be worshipped–nothing or nobody else was to take God's place. Daniel was not going to break God's law–no matter what the punishment was.

When he was caught–and the king's advisors were always watching him, just waiting to catch him, he had to face the punishment. Daniel stood up for what he believed in and was expecting to be thrown into the den of lions–a horrible punishment!

The King liked Daniel and didn't want to punish him, but a law was broken and he had to–especially since the guys that tricked him into doing this would not let him get away with having mercy on someone that broke the king's law. Just before closing the door to the lion's den the king said to him, "I hope your God can save you!"

The next day the king ran to the lion's den. He was amazed when Daniel came out of the den without a scratch on him. The King knew that Daniel's God had saved him and was the one true God. He ordered that everyone in His kingdom respect and honor Daniel's God.

Do you dare to be like Daniel? Do you dare to stand up for what you believe in like Daniel did, despite the consequences?

Discussion #2 (fit in schedule wherever you prefer): "I dare you to accept the ultimate dare–follow Jesus!"

This is a perfect opportunity to offer an invitation to accept Jesus. You need to be ready to offer one at anytime it is appropriate, and you need to be extremely comfortable with the words you use to share it. If you have not done so already prepare, in your own words, the words for your invitation. Remember, it needs to be simple for kids to understand, sincere in

its tone and succinct in its delivery. For an example of an invitation you will find one in the "Salvation Invitation" section of this book.

If anyone accepts your invitation and asks Jesus into their heart for the first time please make it a special celebration with the rest of the group. It's not a time for embarrassment but they should be aware of their awesome step of faith. Tell them that there is a party in Heaven at that moment for the place that has been reserved for them!

Supplies Needed for "Dare" Based on Funds available			
Activity	Budget	Budget w/ some frills	Bells & Whistles
General	-Washcloth for each kid -Cleaning rags -2 Tables -Cones – to designate point for start of relay and for boundaries -Masking tape – for boundary lines -Stopwatch -Trash can -Baby wipes	Same	Same
Pin the Tail	-Donkey (s) -Container(s) with something mushy in it -Blindfold (s) -Marker	Same	Same
Dirty Diaper Relay	-Diapers -Packs of pudding -Spoon (to put pudding on diaper) -Cones -Table	Same plus -Scooters or skateboards	Same

Spamalot	-Cones -Plastic dropcloth (if inside) -Bobbing tubs w/ water -Spam cubes	Same	Same
Jello Slurp and Spit	-Cones -2 Tables or 1 long one -Straws -1 Container of Jello per team – doesn't need to be much in each -1 clear plastic cup per team with a mark ½ way up	Same	Same
Balloon Bottom Squash	-Cones -Water Balloons -Shaving cream -Bucket to put balloons in	Same	Same
Wormalot	-Cones -Bobbing tubs w/ water -Gummy worms	Same	Same
Olive You	-Cones -Masking tape for line -1 cake pan or other target per team -1 jar olives per team	Same	Same
Juicy Juice	-1 tub per team -Grapes (lots) – or peeled oranges -Dixie cups -Fun music -CD player	Same but use kiddie pools instead of tubs	Same
Baby Bottle Chug	-Cones -Table -1 baby bottle per kid w/ slit cut into nipple -Prune juice	Same	Same

Ketchup with Me	-Cones	Same	Same
	-Table		
	-1 Bowl of M&M's covered in ketchup per team		
	-1 spoon per player		
Snoot Shoot	-Cones	Same	Same
	-Masking tape for shooting line		
	-1 target per team		
	-1 pack skittles per team		
Stinky Soda Swig	-Plastic cups	Same	Same
	-Soda		
	-Clean, old socks –if you are nice		
Don't Forget to Brush	-Disposable Plastic dropcloth	Same	Same
	-Blindfolds		
	-1 tube toothpaste per 2 kids		
	-Dixie cups		
Stinky Twinkies	-Twinkies or cupcakes	Same	Same
	-Filler for twinkies – you decide the degree of surprise inside		
	-Table		
Steal the Bacon	-Cones	Same	Same
	-Masking tape or spray paint for lines		
	-Disposable dropcloth		
	-Bacon		
	-Something to make plastic slippery – or slippery and gross, you decide – or re-use dropcloth from before that now has lots of stuff on it.		
Discussion 1	-Bible	Same	Same
	-TV/VCR or DVD player		
	-VHS or DVD of a lion tamer		
Discussion 2	-Bible		

Deception/Illusion

Theme Target:
Teach kids what it means to be deceived by the Master Illusionist and how to protect against his deception.

Golden Nugget:
Satan is the ultimate deceiver and will try to trick you, but He cannot defeat Jesus.

Scripture:
Revelation 20:10 and Romans 8:39 (NIV)

At the beginning of the event inform kids they need to remove their shoes. Provide a laundry basket for them to put them in. During the first activity send a few leaders with the basket of shoes–they will tie them all together by the laces. For shoes with no laces, tie laces through them if possible, otherwise kids with those shoes sit out that activity.

Open with **"Shuffle Your Buns"** and play this as long as you want—if time allows play long enough for every kid to be in the center.

Activity 1: Shuffle Your Buns

Arrange chairs in circle–enough chairs for all players. One player stands in circle. On "Go" the kid in the circle tries to sit on the empty chair. All players sitting in chairs "shuffle their buns from one chair to the next, trying to keep the empty chair moving from one chair to the next before the kid in the circle can sit down. Start with everyone always moving the same direction until they get used to it. Then, if you feel wild, let the player on either side of the empty chair decide who is going to fill it. Be careful–this can get wild and kids start bumping into each other, but, although it is always shifting, there should be an empty chair at all times. Watch out for cheating–some kids will try to sit on two chairs at the same time. This is not allowed.

The "Deception" is in the fact that the empty chair is always moving around. As you describe how to play the game you could throw something like this in to give them a clue about the theme: *The player in the center is trying to sit down and avoid being deceived by the changing location of the empty chair.*

Allow kids to try to guess the theme. This is a very hard one. It will take some time for them to get it, if they actually do.

Activity 2: Shoe Scramble

It will take about ten to fifteen minutes for all shoes to be back on the appropriate feet–some may need to help if knots tightened during the scramble.

Using the shoes that are now tied together inform the kids that you have deceived them. Let them know that you told them they could be shoeless for the evening, when in fact it was all a trick. They do need to put their shoes back on, but first they have to find them and remove them from the pile. Once they have them back on their feet and tied correctly they can return to their seat. The first _____ (whatever number you designate based on the size of your group) gets a prize. The prize should be a "Gobstopper" or some other candy that starts out as one thing and then changes to another.

Allow kids to try to guess the theme before moving on to the next activity.

Activity 3

Watch the first part of "The Swan Princess" approximately fifteen minutes. Watch until you have seen the practice competition for slaying the beast.

Activity 4: Flavor Challenge (allow twenty minutes for this–you'll need some time to distribute all samples, unless made up ahead of time and ready to go)

In this activity the kids will be given samples of several different exotic beverages, water ice or jello and they have to guess what the flavor is. If you choose to do beverages there are a few very unique ones on the market. Jones soda blends some unique flavors. In combination they are hard to guess. If you want to be really deceptive Jones offers a holiday assortment that is really… unique. Their "holiday" line includes cranberry, Brussels sprouts, turkey and gravy, and a few others that cover the traditional turkey dinner. Watch out–they are *nasty*–but you will get some *awesome* reactions from the kids.

You can achieve the same thing with "water ice" by making your own variations: Tomato juice; gravy; corn; anything you can blend and freeze and then scrape and blend again to look like water ice.

If none of these seems to be up your alley try jello. Jello comes in many flavors already and they can be blended to make some great combinations. Or you can work with unflavored jello and add your own flavorings and colors to it. Consider Beef broth as the liquid added to the unflavored jello, or tomato juice again. What about chocolate or peanut butter jello? It would be completely unexpected and quite unusual in that consistency. Be creative but also be careful about food allergies. The more fun you have with it the better it will be as you deceive the kids.

As you give the instructions for this challenge, be sure to work in another clue about the theme, like, *"As you taste the sample and try to guess the flavor, don't be deceived—it could be a combination of flavors and not just one."*

You can use this as your answer sheet, or create your own based on what you are serving them:

Flavor Challenge						
	Sample #	Guess				
	1					
	2					
	3					
	4					
	5					

Flavor Challenge						
	Sample #	Guess				
	1					
	2					
	3					
	4					
	5					

Allow the kids the opportunity to guess the theme. They should be getting close if they haven't already figured it out.

Activity 5:

Watch the climax of "The Swan Princess." Pick up at the point where the fake Odette enters the ball.

Discussion:
How do you prevent being deceived by the Master Illusionist?

If they have not yet figured out the theme now is the time to lead them into it.

Remember at the beginning of the movie, the part when the beast attacks the carriage? Derek comes upon the king and he tells him what happened. The king then warns Derek that the great beast is not what he seems. What is that called when you are deceived because something appears to be one way but it really is completely different?

You are looking for "Illusion"

I have a few illusions to show you and see what you think about them:

You can find way more optical illusions on the Internet than you could possibly use in this event. You will surely find some that you will enjoy sharing with the kids. Simply do a search for "Optical Illusions" through your favorite search engine. One I highly recommend is called the "Jesus Illusion"—which is the term you should search on this one.

Print them out on paper, or for everyone to view at the same time print onto an overhead transparency and use with an overhead projector. If you are more technically savvy, keep them on your computer and show them through a media projector.

Take some time with the illusions—some kids won't get them right away and you want them to get the full effect. The Jesus illusion may take a few tries for some kids, but they will think it is really cool.

From here you move on to the greatest illusionist.

Ask the kids if they have ever seen a magician on television or elsewhere. Get them to explain what a magician does—which is trick you into seeing what they want you to see instead of what is really happening.

That is exactly what Satan does. He wants us to think that God doesn't love us. He wants us to believe that what he has to offer is much better than what God has to offer. He tricked Eve into eating the apple from the tree that she was told by God was off limits. How did he do that? By making her believe that the only reason God didn't want her to have it was because He knew that it would make her equal with God.

Satan is always working to make us believe that God has no power over us and we should not obey God. He is always trying to get us to follow him and turn away from God. He doesn't want us to know how much God loves us. Satan wants us to think that he knows what is best for us.

In reality Satan hates us. He hates anything that loves. He really hates God. The Bible indicates that Satan actually used to be an angel in Heaven. He was considered to be very beautiful and was equal to the highest ranking angels. But his pride got the best of him. He didn't like that he could only do as much as God allowed him to. He thought he should be equal to God. He denied the truth and so, was kicked out of Heaven. So, he hates God and everything and everyone that is associated with God. He now tries desperately to get us to turn our backs on God too–though it's not because he loves us. It's because he hates God.

Satan is the ultimate deceiver. Those who believe him will be doomed to an eternity with him, in hell.

The only way to defeat Satan is with Jesus. With Jesus in your life you will be free from an eternity in hell. The Bible tells us (Revelation 20:10 - NIV) that Satan will be thrown into a lake of fire, which we call hell, to be punished there forever. People who do not believe in Jesus will be in the lake of fire also. By believing in Jesus and asking him into your heart and life you are defeating Satan's attempts to keep you from Jesus. Satan will still try to take you away from Jesus but he cannot separate you from him. The Bible tells us that nothing in all of creation can separate us from the love of God which is in Christ Jesus (Romans 8:39 - NIV)

This is a perfect opportunity to offer an invitation to accept Jesus. You need to be ready to offer one at anytime it is appropriate, and you need to be extremely comfortable with the words you use to share it. If you have not done so already prepare, in your own words, the words for your invitation. Remember, it needs to be simple for kids to understand, sincere in its tone and succinct in its delivery. For an example of an invitation you will find one in the "Salvation Invitation" section of this book.

If anyone accepts your invitation and asks Jesus into their heart for the first time please make it a special celebration with the rest of the group. It's not a time for embarrassment but they should be aware of their awesome step of faith. Tell them that there is a party in Heaven at that moment for the place that has been reserved for them!

Closing activity: Deception Dodgeball
play this game until the end of the event

This is played like normal dodgeball–two teams. The exception here is that each team secretly designates a deceiver. When a player is hit with the ball they sit down where they got hit. The deceiver can revive them by touching them, letting them back into the game as though they were never hit. If the deceiver is hit, all players that were revived by the deceiver are now out for good and so is the deceiver. Play continues until one team has nobody left standing.

Supplies for "Deception/Illusion" Based on Funds available			
Activity	Budget	Budget w/ some frills	Bells & Whistles
Shuffle Your Buns	-Chairs arranged in a circle	Same	Same
Shoe Scramble	-Laundry Basket -Shoes from the kids -Gobstoppers or other prize	Same	Same

Flavor Challenge	-Flavor samples -Plastic Dixie cups for sample -Plastic spoons if water ice or jello -Pencils or markers -Flavor challenge answer sheets	Same	-Flavor samples – use the Jones soda and keep it in the soda bottles, with labels removed and the caps still sealed so they see you haven't done anything weird to the soda to alter its flavor -Plastic Dixie cups for sample -Pencils or markers -Flavor challenge answer sheets
Discussion:	-TV/VCR or DVD player -"Swan Princess" video or DVD -Optical illusions -Overhead Projector	Same	Same
Deception Dodgeball	-Balls (ones that don't hurt when you are hit with them) -Masking tape on the floor to split the room if necessary	Same	Same

Domino

Theme Target:

Teach kids about the effects of lying.

Golden Nugget:

Just like the dominoes continue to fall so did Adam and Eve, and every person since them, except Jesus.

Scripture:

Genesis 1

Separate the group into two teams for the event.

Activity # 1: Tug of War

This is a classic and needs no explaining. Tie a bandana to the center of the rope and put masking tape marks on the floor to aid in determining the winner. The team that pulls the bandana past the mark wins the game. For an added challenge you could do this outside and have a baby pool as the mark and the kid in the front of the losing line ends up wet–just make sure the kid in the front of the line is a good sport. For fun, put the kids in their lines before bringing out the baby pool.

Activity #2: Catch Me if You Can

Put a line of masking tape down the center of the room.

Instruct the members of the largest team to get a chair and bring it to the center of the room. You will create a line of chairs, set up like musical chairs with them alternating the direction they face. There should also be one and a half chair widths in between each of them. Leave as much room as possible at the ends of the line without crowding your chairs too close. Finally, take away one chair, so there is one for each team member minus one (the remaining player is the chaser).

The other team is to line up against the wall, in whatever order they choose. They will run in that order.

It should look like this:

LINE OF WAITING RUNNERS

LOCATION TO SIT WHEN TAGGED

The team in the chairs is "it" while the other team is being chased, one at a time.

Instruct the team that got the chairs to sit down on them, keeping their feet in **front** of the chair–an important safety rule to prevent a fall from accidental or intentional (if intentional, discipline is necessary) tripping. Select one member to be the first chaser.

Now for the tricky part… We'll start with the team being chased.

The team that is being chased will release one player at a time. That player can run anywhere in the playing court–around the ends of the chairs, through the gaps between the chairs and anywhere on either side. The rest of the team stays in their line, waiting for their turn to run. Those waiting must keep one foot against the wall at all times (this is for safety purposes as it keeps them close to the wall. Trust me the line will drift away from the wall so the kids can see what is going on. This cuts down on the running space and creates safety issues).

The kid that is being chased runs as long as possible without being tagged by the other team's runner. Once tagged the chaser immediately goes to work on catching the next runner. The next runner needs to begin running immediately so they have a better chance of getting away. A leader will need to stand at the head of the line and watch for the runner to get tagged and notify the next runner to "GO." The team being chased must pay attention so they are ready for their turn. Also, the runner being chased needs to make sure they do not get tagged close to the rest of their team. If tagged too close to the line, the chaser can easily go right down the line tagging each new player before they even get a chance to run.

Instruct the players that once tagged they are out and must sit or stand against the wall on the other side of the room.

The team that is "It" must only have one person running at a time, that runner is the chaser. Unfortunately, the chaser can only chase on one side of the chair line. If the runner crosses the line, either by running around it on either end or by running through it in a gap between chairs, the chaser must tap the shoulder of one of his teammates that is sitting in a chair facing the side that the runner is now on. The chaser cannot cross over the line. Once a new chaser is tapped and leaves their chair the retired chaser sits in the now empty seat and waits to be tapped again.

Keep a stopwatch running during each round. The team that lasts longer without all being tagged wins the round. The kids will want to play several rounds.

If this is the first time you are playing this game there are two important things to do:

1. Run the first round slowly so the kids get the hang of it. It may take the entire first round for them to remember to only run on their side, to use the gaps in the chairs, to not run full steam if it is not necessary (I have seen savvy kids eat up lots of time by not

running much at all but, rather, just staying close to the chair line and crossing over far enough to be out of reach—utilizing the rule for chasers to not cross over).

2. Realize that this will not be the last time you play this game

Be aware that you may use a lot of time explaining this game. It is difficult to explain without using examples, but once the kids know how to play it is a blast and will surely become a favorite.

Activity #3: Domino Rally

Start by watching the scene in Robots where they accidentally set into motion the dominoes that are set up in BigWeld's house.

Have the kids break up into smaller groups. Give each group a bunch of dominoes to work with and a designated area to work with them. Also give them paper and pencil to create a design to work from. Remind them that they should be creative with curves and tricks. You could also design some patterns for them, if you choose to give them something to work with.

Give each group a push-pin, balloon, a short ruler and some tape. Tell them that those tools are for the grand finale, if they choose to attempt it. The trick is that their last domino has the ruler taped to the domino and a push-pin taped to the top of the ruler and when it falls the pin pricks the balloon, which they have blown up and taped down so the pin can reach it to prick it.

Note: This works better on a non-carpeted floor—even if it is industrial carpet. If you only have carpet—No Worries—consider laying an eight-foot table on the floor for each group to work on.

Suggest that periodically they leave gaps in the display and then fill them in later. This will help prevent losing the entire display in case of a domino falling over.

Instruct them to work as a team to set up their domino displays. They will be given a specified amount of time–but don't tell them how much time. When time is up each display will be judged on the following criteria before set into motion:

1. Difficulty
2. Creativity
3. Number of dominoes used
4. Teamwork
5. Tricks

Discussion: The Domino Effect

Open the discussion with a comment about how well they did on their domino displays.

Ask if they came up with a strategy for creating the display to prevent problems.

Did anyone have a good portion of your display done and one domino fell over and started the whole line going? Did you try to stop it before they all fell down? Were you successful in your attempt?

Have you ever heard of the "Domino Effect?" (You may actually get an answer you can work off of here)

The Domino Effect is exactly what you saw in the scene we watched from Robots. All the dominoes were set up perfectly. One false move set one of them in motion and it started a chain reaction. All the dominoes fell over–pretty rapidly–and there was no stopping them. That term is used to describe any chain reaction that takes place like the dominoes falling.

Have you ever told a lie and then tried to cover it up? Or, have you ever done something you knew you would get in trouble for but made an excuse or blamed something or someone else? What happens in these situations?

Sometimes you get away with it but then you have to live with the guilt. Usually you spend a lot of time trying to cover it up–adding to your story again and again–trying to get the details right every time and not be found out. If you are found out trouble is sure to be the result. Wouldn't it actually be better to just take the punishment? Better yet would be to not do the deed that you are attempting to cover up in the first place.

Is that realistic? It's our nature to sin, isn't it? We get that from a long line of sinners–all the way back to Adam and Eve. That would have to be considered the ultimate Domino Effect.

Pull out a pack of dominoes so you can stand them up as you re-tell the story–or have one of the kids stand them up for you as you instruct them to.

The bible opens with these words: "In the beginning God created the heavens and the earth." (Stand two dominoes on the table–they are your starting point.) You will add a domino for every statement you make). As you are adding dominoes place them in a circle with a tail, to resemble a tree—so that when they are all knocked down you would not be able to tell the beginning or end.

It was dark so God created light.
God separated the water
From the sky
Then God collected the water into specific areas
And provided areas of dry land
Then God had the land produce trees
The trees produced fruit
He made plants that provided food
God then created the Sun
And the Moon
So there was day and night
God then filled the oceans with fish
And put birds in the sky
Then He put animals on the dry ground

God decided to make man to rule over all of the other creatures so He created the first man, in His own image. He called Him Adam.

He decided that Adam needed a companion, so from Adam He created the first woman. He called her Eve.

He gave them a beautiful place to live, which was the Garden of Eden–a paradise.

They had everything they needed.

God told Adam that he and Eve could eat the fruit from any tree in the Garden, except for the tree of the knowledge of good and evil. They were not allowed to even touch the tree. That was the only thing God told him they could not do.

There was also a tree of life (set this domino in the middle of the circle). This tree produced fruit that allowed them to live forever. Imagine living forever!

Your dominoes should look something like this:

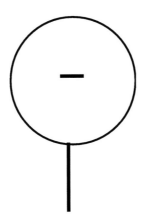

Be sure your dominoes are close enough to each other to knock them all down but the center one. Add to the tail if your circle is complete but you still have more points to make.

But there was one problem. The serpent was clever and he deceived Eve. He told her that the only reason God said not to touch that tree or eat from it was because God knew that then Adam and Eve would know the difference between good and evil and be just like God.

And Eve believed the serpent. She went to the tree and took some fruit and ate it, and then gave some to Adam. (Set the first domino in motion)

Eve disobeyed God. She did exactly what He told her not to do. When God questioned her she blamed it on the serpent. She didn't take responsibility for her actions. When God asked Adam why he ate the fruit he blamed it on the woman that God made for him. He didn't accept responsibility either. That was the beginning of sin. As you can see–it affected everything they had been given. Except for the tree of life. That was not affected.

God took them out of Eden and made them work for everything. He also decided that since they now knew the difference between good and evil (because they ate from the tree that provided that understanding), they would no longer be able to eat from the tree of life. To eat from that tree would allow them to live forever. He sent an angel and a flaming sword to guard the way to the tree of life–so that no person could eat from it and then live forever.

So Adam and Eve's sin began the Domino Effect of sin. Their sin has been handed down to all the people born since that time–except for Jesus. He is the way to break the Domino Effect and beat the penalty for sin. He became the replacement for the tree of life and all that believe in Him and take Him into their heart can live forever, in Heaven.

Close the discussion with the domino displays. Once everyone has looked at all the displays each group will then take turns setting theirs into motion. Additional points can be awarded for the way they fall based on the following criteria:

1. Whether they all fall
2. Creativity in the fall
3. Difficulty in the set up to make them fall
4. Wow factor at the end

Closing Activity #4: Domino Pick-Up Race

Each group races to pick up their dominoes. The first group that is done and is sitting quietly, wins the game.

Supplies Needed for "Domino" Based on Funds available			
Activity	Budget	Budget w/ some frills	Bells & Whistles
Tug of War	-Rope -Bandana -Masking tape	Same	Same plus a kiddie pool in the center
Catch Me if You Can	-Masking tape for center line -Chairs -Stopwatch	Same	Same
Domino Rally	-TV -VCR or DVD Player -Robots tape or DVD -Dominoes – lots. If you don't have enough through borrowing you can often get a good deal on them by purchasing wholesale on the internet. Also – if you have someone handy you could actually make these yourself. They just need to be uniform in weight so there is no problem knocking them over. -Paper and pencil for each group -Masking tape -1 balloon per group -1 push pin per group -1 ruler or paint stick per group -Prizes for group displays	Same	Same but with more dominoes and then give a pack of dominoes to each kid.
Discussion	-Bible		
Domino Pick Up Race	You already have everything out		

Duct Tape

Theme Target:
Teach kids how to guard their heart.

Golden Nugget:
Duct tape can fix almost anything–but not a heart.

Scripture:
The Armor of God Ephesians 6:10–18 (NIV)

For this night you will need a lot of rolls of duct tape. Fortunately, not all of them will need to be opened so only open them as you need to.

Activity #1: Rip-Off Tag

Everyone puts a piece of duct tape on his or her back. It is every man for him/herself, trying to rip tape off the backs of others and place it on the front of his/her own shirt. Once the tape is off your back you are out.

The kid with the most tape on their front is winner. They can't take the tape off of someone's front.

Activity #2: Duct Tape Fishing

Make a fishing line with the duct tape, as well as a hook (ball of sticky-side out duct tape) and try to remove paper fish from an area.

Give the kids the materials to make their fishing line. On "Go" each team works together to create a fishing line. Once it is created they can begin fishing by throwing out their line to the fishpond and pulling the fish back in. One at a time they will take turns standing at the designated line, without crossing it, and toss their fishing line to the fishpond. Allow two or three tosses per kid for each turn. The first team to have a full basket of fish and is sitting quietly, wins the game.

While the teams are creating their fishing poles you can lay out the fishing pond. The fishpond is simply paper fish laid on the floor at a reasonable distance from the designated point to fish from.

Materials for the fishing poles:

* Some type of rod–short broomstick works great.
* Duct tape–a few rolls per team

With these items they should be working toward a finished product that is the rod with a long line of duct tape attached to it. At the end of the line should be a ball of duct tape with the sticky side out. When they throw out the line a good toss will land the ball in the fishpond and bring a fish back with it.

Note: There is a strong potential for disagreement among teammates on the best way to create the fishing pole. There should be one adult leader among the team to assist them. The leader can be a mediator for problems and also make a suggestion if the kids are at an impasse, but don't allow the leaders to create it for them.

Activity #3: Crowning Achievement or Head Stacker

Crowning achievement:

One kid on the team will place a lightweight roll of duct tape on his head like a crown. He will then begin the passing of the crown. The crown is transferred from one head to the next without using your hands or dropping the roll. If the roll is dropped you decide whether it starts over in the line or moves back one to two heads. It's a blast watching the kids figure out how to do this.

Head Stacker:

With three rolls of lightweight, wrapped duct tape stacked on the first kid's head, he must walk down and around a cone and back. Tag the next player and give the duct tape to them.

The first team that completes the task and is sitting quietly wins the game.

Activity # 4: Duct Tape Bowling

Stand up three to six cups in bowling style–don't do more than six because the leaders that have to re-stack them will be annoyed with it if the kids are actually good bowlers. Give each team three rolls of duct tape–still in the wrapper. Each kid gets three chances to knock down all the cups.

This is not a race. Have each team bowl at the same time. If any teams are uneven then have one kid go twice. For each round the team whose player knocked down the most cups gets one point.

If you want to play a second round you could save time by allowing only one roll per turn.

Activity #5: 3-Legged Taping

Within their teams have the kids pair up. Instruct each pair to duct tape their legs together at the ankles–with the sticky side of the tape out—in this case stronger duct tape is better, or they will need to wrap it around several times. If kids are not wearing pants give the option to not play this one.

All pairs line up on a line at the same time. If space does not allow for this you can run them in heats. On "Go" all pairs run down to the opposite side of the room and back. First team to have all players cross the line wins the round.

You may have some agile kids that think they are smart and can hop the entire way. This is cheating and don't allow it–but feel free to let them try it and call it a "false start" or a "do-over" after they get back to the line, because it's pretty clever and fun to watch. You may also have a pretty mismatched team of big kid with a little kid. They may need to resort to a creative tactic to achieve the goal. You decide what crosses over into cheating.

Activity #6: Looney Ballooney

Give each team a roll of duct tape and thirty balloons. On "Go!" have members of each team roll the duct tape (sticky side out) around one of their teammates below the neckline–*not too tight!* Next, have kids blow up their balloons as quickly as they can and stick as many as possible to the taped-up team member. When the balloons have been attached, the player runs down and around a cone and back to their team. Balloons that fall off during the race can't be re-attached. The team whose player has the most balloons still attached and their player cleaned up and sitting quietly wins the game.

Discussion: Since duct tape won't protect you from Satan or fix you, arm yourself with God's Armor.

Assistant in discussion should dress like a handyman/repairman. He/she should carry a toolbox with an ample supply of tools, including a few rolls of duct tape. You should have a few broken items that he sizes up and decides to fix with Duct Tape. The items should be in plain view of the kids. Suggestions: hem a piece of cloth; fix a broken chair leg; fix a wooden spoon handle; or tape the back of a picture frame to fix it.

DL should begin discussion by asking, "Why do you think our theme is Duct Tape?"

What are some things that you can use Duct Tape for?

As the answers are winding down the Discussion Leader will begin to ask how duct tape can protect you from Satan's tricks and be interrupted by Mr. Fix-It entering the room and walking up to you.

FI: *Sorry to interrupt your group activities. I was called to make a few repairs and this is the only time I could schedule it in. Do you know where everything is? (Looks around and sees the area) Never mind, I see it.*

Don't worry; you won't even know I'm here.

<FI goes over to begin working. He creates quite a scene by pulling everything out to begin the repairs.>

DL: *(To the kids) Where were we? Oh, yes, does anyone have any ideas about how Duct Tape can protect you from Satan's tricks and lies?*

FI: *Sorry to interrupt again, but can I get someone to hold this for me while I repair it?*

<Let a kid assist>

FI: *Thank you very much.*

Ummm... could I get someone else to help me with this item?

<Let a kid assist>

—This continues for a few items—as long as you feel it should to get the point across—

DL: *Mr. Fix-It, do you always use duct tape for repairs?*

FI: *You'd be amazed what duct tape can do. People use duct tape for all kinds of projects. They use it to make repairs, to hang stuff on the walls, to make things with. Why, I use duct tape for just about everything.*

(Pull out a few copies of things you can do with duct tape if you have them–you can always find plenty of things people have used duct tape for on the Internet)

Even my_____ is made of duct tape (he should show something that has been covered with duct tape or made with it—shoes, wallet, and tools).

*One time I took my horse to the vet because he had a bad foot. My **vet told me to use duct tape on the bottom of the horse's foot after it was bandaged. The tape provided help in securing the bandages and also gave a stronger covering under the hoof for the horse to walk on. That made the bandage* *last a lot longer.* (**This has actually happened in the world of veterinary medicine so you are not making this up)

DL: *That's amazing. People actually use it for bandages. I knew the stuff was good for a lot of things, but...*

FI: *Sure is. I don't go anywhere without it. It even saved my life once!*

DL: *You're kidding. How did duct tape save your life?*

FI: *I was called to fix a thermostat in a walk-in freezer at a meat packing company. I was in the freezer working and my watch stopped working so I didn't know what time it was. Meanwhile, the workday ended and everyone went home. The last person to leave is supposed to lock the freezers and refrigerators, which he did, but he didn't know I was still working. So, I finished my work and was ready to leave–but I couldn't get out of the freezer.*

DL: *You were locked in for the night?!? That's terrible. So, you used the duct tape to get out of there?*

FI: *Nope!*

DL: *You taped the cooling unit?*

FI: *Nope!*

DL: *How in the world did the duct tape save your life then?*

FI: *I had a few rolls of duct tape in my tool kit–I always have a few rolls in my toolkit. I wrapped the duct tape around me, from my toes, all the way up to the top of my head.*

DL: *You duct taped your head?*

FI: *I was wearing a hooded sweatshirt and pulled the hood up over my head and around my face and tied it so that only a little hole was open–that was my breathing hole. The duct tape **kept me insulated and warm until the next morning. One of the employees found me there, sound asleep and warm as could be. Not only did I survive, I didn't even get one spec of frostbite on me.*

(***In case you are wondering this would actually work. The problem would be whether there would be enough oxygen for the person to survive; however, since that is not the problem, then don't mention it. If a kid asks you just reply that it was an extremely large freezer and plenty of air for one person for that length of time.)

DL: *Wow! Duct tape really is amazing. It can actually protect you from freezing to death or getting frostbite.*

FI: *Well, I'm done with all my repair work. I am sorry I interrupted your discussion.*

        I'll be on my way but first, in answer to your question about how it can protect you from Satan's tricks and attacks–it can't!

DL: *You're right. I forgot I asked that question, I was so caught up in your story. Thank you for bringing us back to that.*

FI: *No problem. So long kids!*

DL: *Wow! Amazing.*

        He's right about not being able to protect yourself from Satan with duct tape.

        Anyone know how to do that?

        The Bible tells us to put on the full armor of God.

Open your Bible to Ephesians 6 and read verses 10–18 (NIV or The Message).

There you have it–duct tape cannot protect you from the evil one, but God can. He has given you a full set of protective armor to wear. It is not physical armor–you can't touch it. But you will never be any safer than when you have it on.

Explain what each piece of armor is and how to put it on:

Belt of truth buckled around your waist—Knowing the truth of God— His existence, His love for His people, His presence

Breastplate of righteousness—the righteousness of Jesus in you. Having Him in your heart is your breastplate

Feet fitted with the readiness that comes from the gospel of peace.–Inner peace from the presence of Christ

Shield of faith—living by the faith that God is with you–allowing you to extinguish all the flaming arrows of the evil one.

Take the helmet of salvation–knowledge of God's love and saving grace–His Salvation

Sword of the Spirit - the word of God.

Prayer in the Spirit on all occasions with all kinds of prayers and requests. With this in mind, be alert and always keep on praying for all the saints.

The best way to put on your armor is by: accepting Christ as your Savior and then have a relationship with Him by reading the Bible and talking to Him. As you do this you will be armed and ready to live for Him.

Closing Activity: Duct Tape Bridge

Set up two chairs per team, five feet apart and with the seats facing away from each other. Give each team two or three rolls of duct tape. On "Go" they work together to build a bridge with duct tape on the folding chairs before you yell, "Stop!" Once all building stops each team selects one kid to sit on the bridge and two other kids–one to sit on either chair. On "Go" the team can help place the kid on the bridge but must then step away from them. Now wait and see which team can have the kid sit on it the longest–with only the bridge to sustain them. No teammates are allowed to help them in any way. If the bridge fails or the kid falls off they are done.

Note: Don't tell them how much time they have–you gauge it as they are building and end it when you feel appropriate.

Supplies Needed for "Duct Tape" Based on Funds available			
Activity	Budget	Budget w/ some frills	Bells & Whistles
Rip-off tag	-Duct tape	Same	Same
Looney Ballooney	-Balloons (lots) -Duct Tape -Cones -Scissors (to remove the tape)	Same	Same

Duct Tape Fishing	-Duct Tape -Paper fish cutouts -2 broom sticks – cut one in half -Cones -Masking tape for lines -Scissors for each team -Basket or bucket for each team to collect their fish.	Same	Same
Duct Tape Bowling	-Rolls of duct tape – still wrapped in plastic -Plastic cups or cones to set up as "pins" -Cones and masking tape for fault line	Same	Same
Crowning Achievement	-1 roll of duct tape per team - still wrapped in plastic	Same	Same
Head Stacker	-3 rolls of duct tape per team – still wrapped in plastic -Cones	Same	Same
3-Legged Taping	-Duct tape -Cones or masking tape for end lines	Same	Same
Discussion	-Actor -Items in need of repair that duct tape can fix -Toolbox with full set of tools -Several rolls of duct tape in toolkit -Bible	Same	Same
Duct Tape Bridge	-2 chairs per team -3 rolls of duct tape per team	Same	Same

Extreme

Theme Target:
Teach kids about the extreme challenge to follow Christ and the extreme rewards.

Golden Nugget:
Will you be an Extreme Christian?

Scripture:
Daniel 3 - Shadrach, Meshach and Abednego

The number of activities in this event allow for several hours of time. Pick and choose what you prefer if this is not for an all-day block. Some of the activities require very nice weather and to be outside.

Kids should be forewarned to wear old clothes and sneakers and to have a towel and change of clothes for their ride home.

Separate the kids into two teams for the entire event. Within the teams, starting with the smallest kid, assign each player on each team a number, one through the highest number of players on the largest team. If teams are uneven select a kid on the smaller team to give a second number to.

Activity #1: Joust Extreme

Set up two overturned buckets, a few feet apart, in the center of the playing area. When you call a number the two players from each team with that number come to the center. They each stand up on a bucket. A leader blindfolds each of them, hands them a pool noodle and faces them in the right direction. You may need to adjust the distance between the buckets based on the reach of the kids. Just for fun, with kids who are good sports, once they are blindfolded move the buckets completely out of reach, or turn both players around so there is no chance of hitting each other.

Always keep them guessing about what you will do next.

Ask each of them individually, "Are you ready to joust?" When you have gotten a "yes" from each one say, "Go!" On "go" they will each try to knock the other one off their bucket with the pool noodle.

This actually sounds more dangerous than it is, but keep a leader close to "spot" each player if you are concerned.

Note: If the pool noodles are long the kids will figure out that they can make a loop with them to wrap around the opposing player. You be the judge of whether you want to allow this.

Also note, if buckets are on a slippery floor they could slide out from under the kid easily.

Activity # 2: Extreme Dodgeball

In this game the leaders get to have a ton of fun throwing balls at the kids. Give each leader a bucket and many balls that don't hurt in their bucket. Splash balls are great because their weight allows them to be thrown a decent distance but they don't hurt. For added fun and if it's a really nice day, put water in the buckets and use them as actual splash balls to get the kids wet. Talk about *extreme!!*

Split up the leaders so you have a few on both sides of the playing area–which should be a rectangle, with a line at each of the ends.

All the kids, no matter what team, should line up at one end of the playing area. Set up cones to designate the corners. On "GO" the kids must all run to the other end of the playing area. The leaders try to hit the kids by throwing the balls at them. Every player that makes it across the other end line stays in to go again. Any player that receives a direct hit before he crosses the line at the other end must sit down where he got hit. He now becomes an obstacle for the remaining kids to get past.

If your playing area is extremely large you could allow the ones that are sitting to be more than just obstacles–they could be taggers. While they must remain sitting and in their spot they could tag a player as he runs by and it be equivalent to a direct hit from a leader.

Play as many rounds as it takes to get down to one kid. The team that the last player represents receives points.

Play as long as you want or until the kids are growing tired of it– which will take a while.

Note: Be sure to use balls that don't hurt if a kid is hit in the face or head so you can avoid needing the rule that they must be hit from the neck down. Kids will cheat on this one if given an opening to do so.

Activity # 3: Extreme Lawn Mower Relay (must be played outside–don't do this if the bees are bad in your location)

One by one each team member will run down to the designated area where they will find a pair of scissors in a shallow container. They must pull out the scissors and take a grass clipping. They then put the grass into the intended container. They then replace the scissors in their container, run back to their team and tag the next player. The catch is that the scissor container has enough syrup, or sticky substance, to cover the scissors.

The team that collects the most grass after one or two rounds (you decide how many times they have to go), is sitting quietly, wins the game. You could have a two-part challenge here–the team that completes the task the fastest and the one that collects the most grass.

Activity # 4: Extreme Wrestling (Sumo Tube)

Make a square–approximately 12' x 12' to use as the playing area. Each team should be standing or sitting well outside of the playing square.

When you call a number the kid on each team that has that number comes to the center. You will give each one of them an inner tube and have them hold it around their waist. Once "tubed" up insist that they honor their opponent by bowing (you will have some kids that really play this up and bow like a sumo wrestler would—which is great fun).

Ask each one, individually, "Are you ready to rumble?" When you have received a "yes" from each one yell, "GO!"

On "go" they will each try to push the other one out of the playing area with their inner tube. They must keep both hands on the tube at all times so as not to push or hit with their hands. If a fall occurs pause the play and let the fallen player get up and reset.

The first player to step over the line of the playing box, if even just a toe, is the loser and both return to their team.

The kids will LOVE this game; and after all of them have gone, they will most likely ask if they can challenge a specific player. Allow this as you have time and as long as the other player accepts the challenge.

Activity # 5: Extreme Tag (Catch Me If You Can)

Put a line of masking tape down the center of the room.

Instruct the members of the largest team to get a chair and bring it to the center of the room. You will create a line of chairs, set up like musical chairs with them alternating the direction they face. There should also be one &½ chair widths in between each of them. Leave as much room as possible at the ends of the line without crowding your chairs too close. Finally, take away one chair, so there is one for each team member minus one (the remaining player is the chaser).

The other team is to line up against the wall, in whatever order they choose. They will run in that order.

It should look like this:

LOCATION TO SIT WHEN TAGGED

The team in the chairs is "it" while the other team is being chased, one at a time.

Instruct the team that got the chairs to sit down on them, keeping their feet in **front** of the chair–an important safety rule to prevent a fall from accidental (or intentional–if intentional, discipline is necessary) tripping. Select one member to be the first chaser.

Now for the tricky part… We'll start with the team being chased.

The team that is being chased will release one player at a time. That player can run anywhere in the playing court–around the ends of the chairs, through the gaps between the chairs and anywhere on either side. The rest of the team stays in their line, waiting for their turn to run. Those waiting must keep one foot against the wall at all times (this is for safety purposes as it keeps them close to the wall. Trust me the line will drift away from the wall so the kids can see what is going on. This cuts down on the running space and creates safety issues).

The kid that is being chased runs as long as possible without being tagged by the other team's runner. Once tagged the chaser immediately goes to work on catching the next runner. The next runner needs to begin running immediately so they have a better chance of getting away. A leader will need to stand at the head of the line and watch for the runner to get tagged and notify the next runner to "GO." The team being chased must pay attention so they are ready for their turn. Also, the runner being chased needs to make sure they do not get tagged close to the rest of their team. If tagged too close to the line the chaser can easily go right down the line tagging each new player before they even get a chance to run.

Instruct the players that once tagged they are out and must sit or stand against the wall on the other side of the room.

The team that is "It" must only have one person running at a time, that runner is the chaser. Unfortunately, the chaser can only chase on one side of the chair line. If the runner crosses the line, either by running around it on either end or by running through it in a gap between chairs, the chaser must tap the shoulder of one of his teammates that is sitting in a chair facing the side that the runner is now on. The chaser cannot cross over the line. Once a new chaser is tapped and leaves their chair the retired chaser sits in the now empty seat and waits to be tapped again.

Keep a stopwatch running during each round. The team that lasts longer without all being tagged wins the round. The kids will want to play several rounds.

If this is the first time you are playing this game there are two important things to do:

1. Run the first round slowly so the kids get the hang of it. It may take the entire first round for them to remember to only run on their side, to use the gaps in the chairs, to not run full steam if it is not necessary (I have seen savvy kids eat up lots of time by not running much at all but, rather, just staying close to the chair line and crossing over far enough to be out of reach—utilizing the rule for chasers to not cross over).

2. Realize that this will not be the last time you play this game

Be aware that you may use a lot of time explaining this game. It is difficult to explain without using examples, but once the kids know how to play it is a blast and will surely become a favorite.

Discussion: Being an Extreme Follower of Christ

Show a video of an Extreme Sports competition.

After the video clip ask the kids, "Who here is into extreme sports? What is your favorite to participate in or watch?"

Those things are very thrilling–and dangerous–which is where the thrill comes from.

The Bible is full of stories of extreme challenges. Some are about people needing to fight against overwhelming odds–like a young boy battling a giant, or a strong man knocking down a temple with his bare hands, or even a small army of men knocking down a solid wall that protected a city and it's army.

But there are also stories of standing up for what you believe in despite the threat of an extreme punishment. That happened with a man who continued to pray to God instead of a king and he was tossed into a den of hungry lions as his punishment. God protected him and the lions didn't eat him, but there is another EXTREME story that involved three guys that were friends.

Their names were Shadrach, Meshach and Abednego. They were three guys that wanted to serve God and obey his commandments. The King at that time was very arrogant. With a name like "Nebuchadnezzer" you wouldn't think he would be, but he was. I bet he was called "Nezzie" as a kid. Anyway, he wanted everyone to bow down to him and worship him. He even had a huge gold statue made that the people in the kingdom had to bow down to when music played–in honor of him.

But Shadrach, Meshach and Abednego refused to do it. They knew it was wrong because God had commanded that only God be worshipped–no person or image was to take God's place. These guys were not going to disobey God, no matter what the law stated the punishment was for it.

Unfortunately, the punishment was really extreme. The law said that if anybody broke the king's command to bow down and worship the statue they would be thrown into a blazing furnace of fire. Forget being grounded—they had horrible punishments in the Bible!!

When Shadrach, Meshach and Abednego refused to bow down there were people that saw it. The people that saw it hated them because they were Jewish and obeyed God's laws over all others. So, they told on Shadrach, Meshach and Abednego. They told the king that they refused to honor him and that he should be embarrassed.

From this point, the story in the Bible goes like this–in Daniel 3:13–23 (The Message):

> Furious with rage, Nebuchadnezzar summoned Shadrach, Meshach and Abednego. So these men were brought before the king, and Nebuchadnezzar said to them, "Is it true, Shadrach, Meshach and Abednego, that you do not serve my gods or worship the image of gold I have set up? Now when you hear the sound of the horn, flute, zither, lyre, harp, pipes and all kinds

of music, if you are ready to fall down and worship the image I made, very good. But if you do not worship it, you will be thrown immediately into a blazing furnace. Then what god will be able to rescue you from my hand?"

Shadrach, Meshach and Abednego replied to the king, "O Nebuchadnezzar, we do not need to defend ourselves before you in this matter. If we are thrown into the blazing furnace, the God we serve is able to save us from it, and he will rescue us from your hand, O king. But even if he does not, we want you to know, O king, that we will not serve your gods or worship the image of gold you have set up."

Then Nebuchadnezzar was furious with Shadrach, Meshach and Abednego, and his attitude toward them changed. He ordered the furnace heated seven times hotter than usual and commanded some of the strongest soldiers in his army to tie up Shadrach, Meshach and Abednego and throw them into the blazing furnace. So these men, wearing their robes, trousers, turbans and other clothes, were bound and thrown into the blazing furnace. The king's command was so urgent and the furnace so hot that the flames of the fire killed the soldiers who took up Shadrach, Meshach and Abednego, and these three men, firmly tied, fell into the blazing furnace.

"It may have looked something like this. (Now show a video clip of an extremely hot furnace–like a glass blowing or steel making documentary–something that focuses on the actual furnace.) Nobody could survive in there–who would even want to?"

But the story in the Bible continues...

Then King Nebuchadnezzar leaped to his feet in amazement and asked his advisers, "Weren't there three men that we tied up and threw into the fire?"

They replied, "Certainly, O king."

He said, "Look! I see four men walking around in the fire, unbound and unharmed, and the fourth looks like a son of the gods."

Nebuchadnezzar then approached the opening of the blazing furnace and shouted, "Shadrach, Meshach and Abednego, servants of the Most High God, come out! Come here!"

So Shadrach, Meshach and Abednego came out of the fire, and the satraps, prefects, governors and royal advisers crowded around them. They saw that the fire had not harmed their bodies, nor was a hair of their heads singed; their robes were not scorched, and there was no smell of fire on them.

Then Nebuchadnezzar said, "Praise be to the God of Shadrach, Meshach and Abednego, who has sent his angel and rescued his servants! They trusted in him and defied the king's command and were willing to give up their lives rather than serve or worship any god except their own God. Therefore I decree that the people of any nation or language who say anything against the God of Shadrach, Meshach and Abednego be cut into pieces and their houses be turned into piles of rubble, for no other god can save in this way."

How amazing would that have been to look into the furnace and see the three men, untied and walking around, with a 4th man that nobody put there—in the hottest fire possible? Then, to not even have them smell like smoke when they came out—AWESOME!!

It doesn't get any more extreme than that! Well, actually it does. That fire is just what hell will be like—and anyone that does not believe in the God of the Bible will spend eternity there, instead of Heaven. Once in Hell there will be no way to be saved—but you can be saved now.

This is a perfect opportunity to offer an invitation to accept Jesus. You need to be ready to offer one at anytime it is appropriate, and you need to be extremely comfortable with the words you use to share it. If you have not done so already prepare, in your own words, the words for your invitation. Remember, it needs to be simple for kids to understand, sincere in its tone and succinct in its delivery. For an example of an invitation you will find one in the "Salvation Invitation" section of this book.

If anyone accepts your invitation and asks Jesus into their heart for the first time please make it a special celebration with the rest of the group. It's not a time for embarrassment but they should be aware of their awesome step of faith. Tell them that there is a party in Heaven at that moment for the place that has been reserved for them!

Activity # 6: Extreme Painting

Provide each kid with a pair of new, white socks (to symbolize following or walking with Jesus) that have been washed once. Allow them to paint their socks in an Extreme Way–you decide how extreme you will let them be.

* If they are inside they should either put them on the arm that is not their painting hand and paint them one at a time or lay them down on the table. The table should be completely covered in newspaper or plastic and have a dropcloth on the floor underneath. Provide a paintbrush for each kid and some extreme colors (fluorescent is great) of paint that won't wash out of the socks but won't make them too stiff to wear.

* If you are up for it and have the space outside lay down a disposable plastic dropcloth. Put some extreme colored paint in some aluminum cake pans. Instruct the kids to put their socks on. At this point you can give them brushes or allow them to finger paint their socks—if they are finger painting remind them that the paint may not wash off quickly—have alcohol and pads or alcohol swabs to assist in removing the paint.

For an added touch play some fun Christian music during this activity.

Activity # 7: Extreme Combat (play outside)

You could do this a bunch of different ways depending on: weather; your budget or the level of mess you want on your hands. Here are a few different suggestions:

Toilet paper combat:

Provide a few rolls of toilet paper and one or two buckets of water to each team. Play just like dodgeball but they make balls out of a few squares of toilet paper dipped in the water and squeezed into a ball. If the ball is still dripping it is more fun.

Water balloon combat:

Have enough water balloons in a bucket to play a few rounds of this.

Each team should line up on their side of the playing area.

In the center of your playing area place two water balloons to start the round.

Call out a number. As soon as they hear the number the kid on each team that has that number runs to the center and picks up a balloon as fast as they can. They then attempt to hit the other player with it before they get hit themselves. The first one to get the other one wet wins the round. If dodged it doesn't count as a score.

Q-tip combat:

Provide each kid with ten Q-tips, a pair of tongs and each team a pan of tempera paint (so it washes off their clothes). Each team should have a different color. Give them a few minutes to make their ammunition–they will each dip their Q-tips into the paint. When the time is up take the paint away and give each kid a straw–big enough to fit the Q-tip in but it shouldn't have too much air space beside that–try to find the best size ahead of time. On "Go" each team goes to war for five minutes (or as long as you choose). They each shoot their Q-tips through the straw to the other side.

In the meantime, any Q-tips that make it to the other team's side should be picked up and shot back. The goal is to have as many of your team's Q-tips on the other team's side as you can.

At the end of the time each team polices the area to pick up Q-tips and then counts how many of the other team's Q-tips are on their side.

Scoring is as follows:

The team that has all the Q-tips on their side picked up first wins twenty-five points.

The team with the most Q-tips on the other team's side wins fifty points.

Count the number of paint marks on each kid that are the opposing team's color. The one with the most marks on the opposition wins seventy-five points or whatever number of points necessary to make it a tie (if you like to do that).

Activity # 8: Jello Wrestling or Jello Belly Flop (play outside)

Lay down one old mattress per kiddie pool you will use. Lay a tarp over that mattress. Place a kiddie pool on the tarp. Fill the kiddie pool with "No-Chill Jello." This can be purchased over the Internet. It can be mixed quickly, possibly right in the pool if it has a smooth bottom (the pool, not the mixer), does not require refrigeration and stays set despite temperature. One case of this makes eighteen gallons. It will cost at least $50.00 per case.

A cheaper route that would not be flavored or colored (unless you add that to it) would be to purchase "Guar Gum" powder and mix it with water. This is a serious thickening agent but is completely safe, and edible. It can be found in health food stores or purchased over the Internet. It is usually a few dollars per eight-ounce bottle. Eight ounces will make approximately twenty batches of this—six gallons.

Measure four cups of warm water into a large mixing bowl. *Slowly* (very slowly) stir in two teaspoons of guar gum. This fine powder has a tendency to clump up if it is not stirred into the water slowly. After thoroughly mixing, pour the guar gum mixture into a bucket with a lid for transport. Unfortunately, if you try to make this in bigger batches it is too difficult to mix it properly. It may actually be faster to mix it in batches of two cups water and one teaspoon guar gum powder in a shaker. Try both ways and see which one works better.

If Jello Belly Flop:

Each team lines up according to size–smallest to biggest. They run up to the kiddie pool and do a belly flop. This really isn't a competition unless you want to make it one by having them compete for the best or most creative flop, but it could just be for fun.

If Jello Wrestling it is a great tie in with the discussion of standing your ground when your faith is attacked and you only need one pool but it must be big enough to wrestle in:

Call a number and the kid from each team that has that number steps into the pool. Ask each one, "Are you ready to stand your ground against your opponent?" When both say "yes" you say "go." On "go" each kid tries to knock the other one down. You decide up-front how far down they have to be to be down: one-knee; both knees or hip or buttocks.

Closing Activity: Extreme Race (slip n' slide- an outside activity)

Set up two "Slip 'N Slides or one double "Slip 'N Slide" or two sheets of plastic with a hose constantly running on them. For added fun set them on a hill with a puddling source at the bottom.

The teams line up according to their number, smallest to biggest. Each pair will race to the end of the slip n' slide. Great Fun!

Supplies Needed for "Extreme" Based on Funds available			
Activity	Budget	Budget w/ some frills	Bells & Whistles
Extreme Joust	-2 blindfolds -2 5 gallon buckets -2 pool noodles	Same	Same
Extreme Dodgeball	-Cones -1 bucket per leader -Lots of balls that don't hurt when hit in face	Same	Same
Extreme Lawnmower	-Cones -2 containers to hold scissors -2 pair scissors -2 containers to put grass in -Syrup or other sticky substance	Same	Same
Extreme Wrestling	-Masking tape -2 inner tubes – real or plastic inflatable pool rings	Same	Same

Extreme Tag	-Chairs -Stopwatch -Masking tape for center line (not necessary but makes it easier to put chairs back each round)	Same	Same
Discussion	-Bible -TV/VCR or DVD player -VHS or DVD of Extreme Sports -VHS or DVD of a fiery hot furnace – try a documentary on making steel or glassblowing	Same	Same
Extreme Painting	-1 pair clean white socks per kid -Newspaper or plastic for table -Disposable Plastic Dropcloth -Aluminum pie tins -Extreme colored (fluorescent is great), non-washable paint -Paint brushes -Alcohol and pads or alcohol swabs -Paper towels -CD player -Fun Christian Music for painting	Same	Same
Extreme Combat	Toilet paper combat -1 or 2 Rolls of toilet paper per team -1 or 2 Buckets of water per team	Water balloon combat -Enough water balloons in a container to play several rounds – at least 2 per kid -Cones	Q-tip combat -Cones for center line -Enough Q-tips for 10 per kid -Aluminum pie tins -Tempera paint – 2 colors -Stopwatch

Jello Wrestling or Jello Belly Flop	-1 or 2 kiddie pools depending on which game you will play -1 or 2 mattresses, if belly flop -1 or 2 plastic drop cloths or tarps if belly flop -"Guar Gum" jelly	Same w/ exception -"Guar Gum" jelly with food coloring – color the water then add the guar gum	Same but use -1 case No-Chill Jello per pool (can be purchased on-line. Search for "No-Chill Jello")
Extreme Race	-2 slip n' slides; 1 double slip n' slide or 2 sheets of heavy duty plastic. -1 or 2 hoses with water source – only one is necessary with the double slip 'n slide	-2 slip n' slides; 1 double slip n' slide or 2 sheets of heavy duty plastic. -1 or 2 hoses with water source – only one is necessary with the double slip 'n slide	-2 slip n' slides; 1 double slip n' slide or 2 sheets of heavy duty plastic. -1 or 2 hoses with water source – only one is necessary with the double slip 'n slide

Fear Factor

Theme Target:
Challenge kids to conquer their fears.

Golden Nugget:
God is with us when we are afraid and He calms our fears.

Scripture:
Exodus 14 - The parting of the Red Sea

This theme is meant to make the kids fearful about the activity they are challenged to participate in. You will have kids that are completely freaked out–you want this to happen. You get to really play it up and freak them out as much as possible. You will also have kids that seem fearless and will readily volunteer to participate in all of the activities. You also want this. The cool thing is that you will have both extremes–which you will want to draw into your discussion time.

This is a very messy event. Warn parents and kids ahead of time that they will need to wear old clothes and bring towels–but don't tell them why, you want the element of surprise. You should have no problem getting additional help for this event if you need it. It promises to be unbelievably fun for them to watch–especially when they are in on all your tricks.

During this event you will be reminded that kids will do just about anything you ask them to do. While this fact will make this event that much more fun it is also a sobering reminder. Keep this in mind in future discussions–especially during the discussion in the "Pressure" theme.

Opening: Show a clip from the opening of the television show "Fear Factor." The opening is suggested because it shows various stunts being attempted in a short period of time. Only show to the main titles–beyond that is not necessary for your event. You can usually find re-runs of this show on various channels. If you don't find it you can show a clip of anything that challenges people to do something they would normally be afraid of.

The kids will have a pretty good idea of the theme at this point. If they've seen the show you will have mixed reactions–boys will be excited and think it's really cool and some of the girls will be a bit freaked already. Now it's time for you to have a blast setting up the expectations for the evening. You want to play this up as big as you can. Perhaps something like this:

"Okay, who has figured out the theme? That's right, it's Fear Factor! We are going to break up into teams and compete to find out who can overcome their fears. Each activity is designed to scare you. It's okay to be scared. Some of you are afraid already, and that's okay. We will use safety precautions so that nobody gets hurt, but be advised, there are some events planned that you will be afraid to participate in."

Get the idea? Trust me, you will have kids that are already freaked out, especially if you have already planned some prior events that were a bit extreme, and if you have already used some of the themes in this book I will assume that your kids have reason to wonder what their attendance at this point has doomed them to.

Anyway, now for the logistical stuff:

Break up into as many teams as necessary to give each kid the opportunity to participate in at least one event. Designate a color for each team. An armband or bandana or something else they can put on their arm that is their team's color would be nice, but not absolutely necessary. Even just one per team would be nice–perhaps a flag or something that each individual participant can bring to their event–but you really only need one since only one team member will participate in each round and they can therefore all share the one team flag, bandana or armband. This is not designed for every kid to participate in each event, but to watch most of them.

Once the teams are set each team member needs to be assigned one number, one through eleven (or whatever number of events you choose to use). The number corresponds with the challenge round. Each kid needs a number but they have no idea what their number is associated with.

Now that they have their number in their team you can explain to them what is going to take place. It should sound something like this:

Each of you has a number within your team. There are eleven challenge rounds. Your number tells you what round you participate in. For example, if you are number seven when I announce that round seven is beginning you will join the other number sevens for your challenge.

Each challenge will be explained once the participants come forward for the round. Once it is explained each person in that round will need to decide whether they are too afraid to participate or not. There is no shame in being too afraid of the challenge, but the points are based on the decision. Here is the point scale:

* If you face the challenge head on and complete it you will earn fifty points for your team.

* If you face the challenge head on but do not complete it you earn twenty-five points for your team.

* If you are too afraid to face the challenge you can select a willing participant from the remaining team members to take your place. The most points that your replacement can earn is twenty for completion. If your replacement attempts but does not complete the challenge only ten points will be awarded for that round. Only one replacement team member is allowed.

* Bonus points–as necessary give bonus points. There are obvious

times for bonus points based on performance in the challenge, but give bonus points for other things like good sportsmanship, encouraging attitude, over*coming a real fear, anything that you feel is necessary–especially if it helps keep scores even.*

Don't be afraid to take points away for bad attitude either.

Example:
Participant #1
Attempts and completes   50 points

Participant #2
Attempts but does not complete   25 points

Participant #3
Assigns replacement who completes   20 points

Participant #4
Assigns replacement who attempts but does not complete   10 points

Participant #5
Assigns replacement that accepts challenge but backs out   0 points

The challenge rounds:

Note: Use as many as you have time for. Each round, with explanation, will take approximately ten minutes to accomplish–start to finish.

If your facility is capable of this it is nice to have each round in a different location–though outside is necessary for some of them.

Round #1: Ping-Pong Ball Retriever

Blindfolded participants pick out three ping-pong balls from plate of live worms with bare feet and put them outside the plate. First one to complete the challenge earns extra bonus points.

Sit contestants down on a chair, all at the same time, and tell them to take their shoes and socks off. As they are doing that inform them of the challenge.

"This challenge requires you to use only your feet. You will feel around for the ping-pong balls on the plate, pull them out with your toes and put them on the ground next to the plate. There's one catch… there are a few extra things on the plate besides the ping-pong balls. (Reveal the plates). Are each of you up to this challenge?"

Blindfold them and say "Go."

Round #2: Fear fall

Blindfolded participants fall backwards from an elevated platform into what they believe is the smallest kid on their team's arms–actually, once blindfolded and turned around adult leaders step in to be the catchers of the kids that are falling. All participants must fall on the count of three. No talking allowed by kids that are watching.

Talkers assessed point penalty for team.

Position the contestants on their platforms.

"We are going to blindfold you and turn you around so your back is to us. Once I count to three, you will fall back into the arms of your teammate (have the leader of each team send the smallest teammate forward to the platform). Your teammate will catch you before you hit the ground… hopefully. Once safely on your feet you have completed the challenge. Anyone want to select a replacement?"

Once the contestants turn around:

"For this challenge the contestants need complete silence. Anyone watching that makes a sound during the challenge will lose thirty points for their team."

"O.K. Go!"

Round #3: Gumball dispenser

Partially fill a shoebox with live mealworms–or some other crawly thing. Show kids contents of the box. Add one gumball (wrapped in plastic) to box for each participant.

"In this challenge contestants must reach their hand into this box to find a gumball. Once located you must pull it out and eat it. Are each of you up to this challenge?"

One at a time have them perform the challenge.

Round #4: Rotten old egg

We all know the egg is fresh but wait until you see how it looks when you finish prepping it.

Hard-boil enough eggs for one per contestant. Peel them and let soak in a mixture of vinegar and black food coloring for a few hours. Black can be purchased in cake decorating section of craft stores or any store that carries cake-decorating supplies. Black can also be achieved by mixing lots of dark colors together. Keep them in the solution and retrieve at time of challenge with a big slotted spoon.

*For those of you who feel this is over the top, just rest assured that the eggs will not harm them one bit. Everything is edible but their minds will cause them to question it.

"In this challenge you will be required to eat a rotten, five-year old egg. You must eat the entire egg to earn the full fifty points for your team. When I say 'Go" you will each begin eating. The first one to finish their egg will earn bonus points for their team. Anyone want to choose a replacement for this challenge?"

Give out all the eggs and say, "Go!"

Round #5: Bobbin' for worms

Take the contestants back to the plates with the ping-pong balls. Instruct the kids that,

"Once blindfolded you will wait for the word 'GO.' When I say 'GO' you will put your face down into the plate and feel around for a worm, then eat it as quickly as possible, without using your hands. The first one to finish earns extra bonus points. "For this challenge the contestants need complete silence. Anyone watching that makes a sound during the challenge will lose thirty points for their team. Are each of you up to this challenge?"

Once the contestants are blindfolded switch the plates with fresh ones that have chopped up cookies and a few gummy worms on them. Wet the gummy worms to make them slippery.

"OK. Go!"

Round #6: Shake it up

Using a blender, make a big deal as you mix the following ingredients:

* A handful of the worms and dirt from challenge #1

* Spoiled milk poured from a carton–either plan ahead and let milk spoil in the carton so it is clumpy and use that or mix cottage cheese into milk in the carton. Clumpy is a necessary effect.

* Sardines or some other nasty looking food that freaks kids out– the whole sardines get a fun reaction.

* Chocolate syrup

* Blend this up in front of all the kids–make it as smooth as possible.

* Once blended take them to a new area and have a leader bring you either an identical looking blender pitcher with the good milkshake in it or a cup of milkshake for each contestant.

* Ingredients for good milkshake, made up ahead of time:

  Milk, Oreo cookies, a little chocolate syrup, neutral colored gummy worms or gumdrops

Pour milkshake into cups in front of the kids.

"When I say 'Go' you will each drink your shake as fast as you can. First one done wins Bonus points. Are each of you up to this challenge?"

Round #7: Dumpster Diver

Contestants will dig through trash with bare hands to find an item in a Ziploc bag. They must pull the item out, remove it from its bag and then eat two bites of it.

Use a brand new trashcan and "clean" trash–be creative with this part–a few of the meal worms from before added to the top would be a nice effect. A little vinegar in the trash can will make things smelly and wet and get you a great reaction.

Suggested items in the bags that they need to find and eat:

Banana that has some nice brown spots on it; cut apple that has browned; bologna sandwich with mustard smeared a bit on edges, torn up to look partially eaten. Be creative here–presentation is everything, even though you know what they are eating is perfectly safe.

"In this challenge you will each take turns picking through this trash to find an item in a sealed plastic bag. Once you find one you must remove the item from the bag and eat two *bites of it completely. Are each of you up to this challenge?"*

Have them go, one at a time.

Round #8: Hot, Hot HOT!

Contestants eat a spoonful of diced jalapeno pepper, with the seeds.

You think this has gone too far but, again, appearance is everything but nobody will get hurt in any way, they will just think they will.

Inform the contestants:

"In this challenge you will be required to eat one spoonful of hot pepper entirely, in order to get full credit for the challenge."

At this stage in the competition the kids will definitely be on to you and will think it's going to be a breeze. But you are going to trick them pretty good.

Pull out one whole, fresh jalapeno pepper per contestant. Cut a small piece off of each one.

Now state: *"I know that these are extremely hot peppers and before you decide whether you are going to do this challenge you can touch your tongue to a cut piece of it and see if you think you can handle it."*

You hold the big piece of pepper (don't let them touch it–they could touch it with fingers and then touch eyes later and that really burns) and let them touch their tongue to it–just the tip of their tongue; don't let it touch their lips.

Tell them that you don't want them to be heroic and then regret it because these peppers get extremely hot. Let them know that this is the one challenge that each potential contestant can get a feel for before committing to it, and you will allow more than one replacement, if necessary. Make a fresh cut for each replacement. Be dramatic, but don't lay it on too thick.

Once you have your contestants ready, pull out the baggie or container with the diced green bell pepper in it (look for the darkest green bell pepper you can find)–include a few seeds for visual effect–you will be amazed how much diced green bell pepper looks like diced jalapeno. Scoop a spoonful for each of the contestants and tell them to wait for the "GO" signal.

"When I say 'GO' each one of you will begin eating your spoonful of pepper. The first one completely done earns bonus points. Are each of you up to this challenge?"

"O.K., GO!"

Round #9: Buried treasure

Contestants will search for three "Starburst" or similar chewy candies in plate of cottage cheese and eat them to complete this challenge. Contestants cannot use hands to do this.

"In this challenge you will search for buried treasure on this plate (reveal the plates). Once you find the treasure you must eat it completely and look for another. You must find and eat three treasures to complete the challenge. You cannot use your hands. Are each of you up to this challenge?"

"Ok, Go!"

Round #10: Balloon of Doom

Fill enough water balloons to allow one per contestant and a few extras in case of premature breakage. Here's the catch, they don't have to be filled with water unless you can't bring yourself to douse them with:

1. Watered down applesauce

2. Watered down tomato sauce

3. Watered down pudding

4. Anything else you deem worthy–being careful not to use anything that will sting eyes if it gets in them.

The challenge:

"Contestants will choose one *balloon from the bucket"*
Note: they can't touch them or look at them closely. Make them stand

a few feet away and select them. Mark each one with a marker to note which contestant selected it.

"One at a time you will stand in that spot marked 'X' (a designated area previously marked) to complete the challenge. I will toss your chosen balloon into the air above you. Your job is to try to catch the balloon. If you actually catch the balloon you will earn bonus points. If you catch the balloon and it doesn't pop you will earn additional bonus points. Are each of you up to this challenge?"

**Note: Fill the balloon full enough to ensure it pops on contact. If it is caught and doesn't pop be prepared for a kid that wants to hurl it back at you.

Round #11: Creepy crawlies

Contestants are blindfolded and they lay down on their backs. All at once each one has the remainder of the earthworms and mealworms poured onto their faces.

"On the count of three you will have the leftover worms poured onto your face. Do not open your mouth or they will crawl or fall in. You must stay still for thirty seconds to complete the challenge. Are each of you up to this challenge?"

"For this challenge the contestants need complete silence. Anyone watching that makes a sound during the challenge will lose thirty points for their team."

"Ok. GO!"

You will actually use cooked macaroni with crumbled cookies in it for effect.

Discussion: How to Deal with Fear

Have kids sit on the floor. Leader of discussion should also sit on the floor with TV and DVD player behind, so visible to kids when ready for use.

So, how many of you have been afraid to do what you were challenged to do so far tonight?

While we're talking about Fear—what are you really scared of?

* Give plenty of time for this. You may find that every kid has something they want to share. You need to be quick on your feet here–some kids may share some inappropriate things they've seen on TV or in movies. Be careful, however, to not completely cut them off or embarrass them–if they've been allowed to see it and it is scary, then you have to deal with it without stifling them. You want them to be comfortable to share.

* As always, be prepared to let the discussion guide you. Don't push your discussion back to what you have planned if what is unfolding in front of you is leading in a different direction. For example–you may be completely prepared to talk about the Israelites being led through their fears of being killed by the Egyptians as well as through the Red Sea but the discussion takes you in a direction in which it is appropriate to talk about the reality of Satan and his desire to get them on his side. For that purpose you will see both discussion tracks here.

Moses story:

I'm going to tell you a story about some people that were terrified because a terrible man and his army were chasing them and they were convinced they were going to die.

—Get out a flashlight and have someone turn out all the lights in the room. Hold the flashlight under your chin like you're telling a ghost story.—

OK, let me set the stage. First of all, this is a true story and the bad man in it is really bad. <Laugh an evil laugh> The people were very scared of him because he had total power over them since they were his slaves. The man was the Egyptian Pharaoh and the slaves were the Israelites. Now, every time I say the name Pharaoh, you respond by saying, "Let My People Go!" Let's try it…

Moses was the leader of the Israelite people and he was trying to get them released from slavery. He went and asked the Pharaoh to <Let My People Go>.

–Either tell them they did well or review their responsibility. Don't let them get away with not taking pride in their work.

Every time that Moses went and asked the Pharaoh to <Let My People Go> he said "No." He was a very stubborn man.

So God made some really nasty things happen to Egypt. Each time Moses went and asked the Pharaoh to <Let My People Go> and he said "NO!" something really bad followed. The first time Moses asked the Pharaoh to <Let My People Go> and he refused God turned all of the water into blood so that the fish died and the Egyptians couldn't drink the water.

The second time that Moses asked the Pharaoh to <Let My People Go> and he refused God sent frogs into Egypt. Not just a few frogs. He sent so many frogs that they were Everywhere! They were in the street, in people's homes, in their ovens, their breadboxes, even their underwear drawers. But the Pharaoh <Let My People Go> still said "NO!"

So God continued to send bad things–they are called plagues in the Bible, by the way.

He covered Egypt in gnats–you know, those really pesky, tiny little bugs. Moses struck the dust on the ground with his staff and all the dust turned into gnats. Think about when you help clean your house and sweep up all the dust. Imagine if that was actually gnats. Now think about how much dust a desert would have on the ground since it's a very dry place. That's a crazy amount of gnats.

The next time that Moses asked the Pharaoh to <Let My People Go> and he said "No!" God sent flies. Flies were everywhere, filling the land, destroying everything. Can you imagine how loud the buzzing must have been?

You would think that surely by then the Pharaoh would <Let My People Go>. But he still refused. He was a bad man and also not very bright.

So God sent a plague on all of the livestock–cows, horses, donkeys, sheep and goats. They all died–except for the ones owned by the Israelites. God never harmed them in any of this.

Still he said no. So God sent boils to cover all of the Egyptians bodies. Do you know what boils are? They are swollen, painful, pus filled bumps that form on hair follicles. Every location on your body that has hair–arms, legs, back of your neck, and your head–you can get a boil. The Egyptians had boils all over them. Nasty stuff, huh?

You would think that by now the Pharaoh would <Let My People Go> for sure.   Nope!

God sent hail. Hail came down all over Egypt and destroyed everything growing in the fields and killed whatever animals were left.

Then God sent locusts. (Shine your flashlight on a picture of a locust if you can find one) These insects were everywhere. They covered the land and made it completely black. They also destroyed everything that was left–leaves on the trees and whatever plants and crops that lived after the hail.

He still said no.

God sent darkness. It was pitch black for three entire days and nights. There was no light anywhere in Egypt. They didn't have streetlights then. God made it completely black so they couldn't even see their hand in front of their face. But there was light where the Israelites were.

He still said no.

Have you been counting how many times God sent something bad to show His power and to get Pharaoh to <Let My People Go>? (Recount them with the kids).

So, nine times God sent a pretty bad plague, and he still said no.

God prepared to send the 10th and final plague. This would be the worst one ever.

He gave specific instructions for the Israelites on how to be safe from this plague and they followed them perfectly. For the last plague God went through Egypt and killed all of the oldest sons of every family, including animals–whatever they had now. Even the prince was killed. Once this happened and his own son was dead he called for Moses. Finally, the Pharaoh <Let My People Go>.

So they went. They packed up everything and they left for a new land– the land promised to them by God.

They made it to the Red Sea and camped. But, even though the Pharaoh <Let My People Go> his anger took over and he called his entire army together. They all went to chase down the Israelites.

But the Israelites were pretty much backed up against the wall when they caught up with them—actually they were backed up against the sea—pretty bad either way. They were sitting ducks! Actually, sitting ducks could have just swum away, but they couldn't do anything.

The people were terrified and they were mad at Moses. They couldn't believe that he would have gone through everything with the plagues and stuff only to be led to the Red Sea to die.

But God had a great plan. He was with them and was not going to let them die. He planned to let the Israelites see just how powerful He was, and that they were completely safe with Him.

Let's watch what He did for them…

— Play the clip from "The Prince of Egypt," at the end, where the Red Sea is parted.

Follow up with: God protected the Israelites and He was always with them, through all the plagues and then at the Red Sea. Just before God parted the sea and the people were terrified Moses reminded them, "Don't be afraid. Stand firm. You will see how the Lord will save you today. Do you see those Egyptians? You will never see them again. The Lord will fight for you. Just be still." That must have been an amazing miracle to witness.

God promises to always be with us too, especially when we are afraid.

Fear discussion track:

If your discussion with the kids takes you in a direction that deals more with serious fears that they have you may want to be prepared with this.

Let them talk about things they are really afraid of. You will find that kids are willing and eager to share these things. It can get out of hand with them wanting desperately to "one-up" the other ones. Know when to allow it and when to cut it off.

When you are ready to regain control lead into the most fearful thing that you can think of. Tell them about a few things that frighten you–kids will be very interested to know that adults can be afraid too. Lead into being fearful about the reality of Satan.

I have had this discussion before and talked about how, as a kid, I would pray at night that I would be protected from bad dreams. I had a lot of them as a kid and they always felt so real. Kids will be able to relate to this. I went on to say that I still have bad dreams every once in a while and wake up feeling like Satan is trying to scare me into joining his team in my dream. I described the feeling very vividly–heart pounding, out of breath, shaking a bit, and actually stiff from being so tense. Scared to death and not knowing what to do only one thing comes to mind at that moment… Pray. Share with them that praying for God to give you peace can provide amazing results. I have never known anyone that said that, as they were praying for peace they felt more afraid or agitated. It always has a calming effect.

Lead this discussion based on your own fears of Satan's reality and how he tries to work. You will probably see some pretty wide eyes and even have some interesting questions. Kids can ask some pretty interesting things in this situation. You may not be prepared for everything, but don't worry, God is with you as you speak and He can guide your responses to accomplish His work. You are a servant of His and you will be amazed at how He can use you. Let Him!

Once your discussion, whichever track it took, is over and you have closed it in prayer–if you have chosen to do so–you can finish up with your last challenge.

Final Round: Firing Squad (do this outside)

Have each leader walk out with a large Super Soaker, or hose. You decide whether they use these or whether they also have a can of silly string behind their back.

Insist that each kid line up, whether against a wall or not, and close their eyes–or blindfold them if you have enough blindfolds.

Once they do that you state:

"In this challenge you will have to face the firing squad! Your leaders are going to shoot you with their guns! When I yell 'Fire' they will shoot for fifteen seconds. When I blow the whistle all fire will cease. Anyone that moves to dodge the shooting will lose seventy-five points for their team."

"One–Two–Three–Fire!"

At the end of this round you announce the winning team. You could offer a prize to the team with the most points. You decide that–often times they don't care about the prize at this point, or don't trust it will actually be a good prize after all they've been through.

Enjoy!

Supplies Needed for "Fear Factor" Based on Funds available			
Round # and Name	Budget	Budget w/ some frills	Bells & Whistles
1. Ping-Pong Ball Retriever	-Blindfolds (1/team) -Chairs (1/team) -Paper plates (1/team) -Earthworms in dirt -3 Ping-pong balls per plate -Container to drop balls into	Same	Same
2. Fear fall	-Blindfolds -Elevated platform for each player	Same	Same
3. Gumball dispenser	-Shoebox with mealworms or other crawly creatures (cut hole in lid of shoebox to reach hand in) -Gumballs wrapped and sealed in plastic	Same	Same
4. Rotten old egg	-Container with hardboiled eggs soaked in black food coloring and vinegar – 1 egg per player -Slotted spoon	Same	Same
5. Bobbin' for worms	-Blindfolds -Paper plates -Chopped Oreo cookies -Gummy worms	Same	Same

6. Shake it up	-Blender	Same	Same as the others but -Blender with 2 pitchers or 2 identical blenders
	-Milk		
	-Chocolate syrup		
	-Oreo cookies		
	-Neutral colored gummy worms or gumdrops		
	-Cups		
	-Earthworms (from before)		
	-Sardines		
	-Spoiled milk or cottage cheese and milk		
7. Dumpster Diver	-Clean trash can	Same	Same
	-"Clean trash"		
	-Ziploc bags		
	-Items to eat in the bags		
	Banana; apple;		
	portion of sandwich		
8. Hot. HOT. HOT!	-1 Whole jalapeno pepper per player	Same	Same
	-Knife		
	-Cutting board		
	-Container or baggie with diced, green bell pepper		
	-Plastic spoons		
9. Buried Treasure	-1 Paper plate / player		
	-Cottage cheese		
	-Unwrapped Starburst candies – 3 per plate		
10. Balloon of Doom	-Bucket	Same	Same
	-Water balloons filled with watered down:		
	tomato juice		
	applesauce		
	pudding		
	yogurt		
	anything that won't sting eyes		
11. Creepy Crawlies	-Blindfolds	Same	Same
	-Containers with cooked macaroni and chopped Oreo cookies		

Discussion	-Bible	Same	Same
	-Flashlight		
	-TV/VCR or DVD player		
	-Prince of Egypt video/DVD		
	-Picture of locust		
Final: Firing Squad	-Super Soaker for each leader or a hose.	Same	Same
	-Cans of silly string, if you choose that route		
General – make up a fear factor tool kit for each team	Cleaning rags	Same	Same
	Trash bags		
	Paper towels		
	Goggles		

Fresh/Spring

Theme Target:
Present the Easter story.

Golden Nugget:
Jesus offers us a fresh start!

Scripture:
John 20:1–18 (The Message)

This is a springtime event–for close to Easter.

Activity #1: Sculpting, Drawing, Humming, Charades

Separate the kids into four teams. Within the teams, starting with the smallest kid, assign each player on each team a number, one through the highest number of players on the largest team. If teams are uneven some kids on the smaller teams will need more than one number.

Each team is to line up on one side of the room. On the other side of the room you will have the Sculpting, drawing and humming supplies which are: one container of Play-Doh per team, one pad of paper and pencil per team, one kazoo per player (or they can just hum with no kazoo if you don't want the added expense–novelty toy stores like U.S.Toy and Oriental Trading Company offer kazoos by the dozen and they are very inexpensive. Sanitize them with alcohol and keep in your supply closet).

You will call a number and each kid with that number will come to the table. They will be asked a question. The first one of the four kids to answer gets to choose what the challenge is–either sculpting an object from the Play-Doh, drawing an object, humming a song or acting out a word or phrase. On "Go" the four kids run back to their teams and begin the challenge. The first team to correctly identify what the kid is sculpting, drawing, humming, or acting out gets a point. A leader should come with every contestant so they know what the correct answer is and can determine when their team has guessed it right. Leader cannot participate in guessing or help in any way though.

The next player that comes to the table brings back any supplies from the last challenge.

Theme-related questions to ask for each round:

1. What is the second season of the year?   -Spring

2. April showers bring what May item?   -Flowers

3. Why do people squeeze bread in the grocery store before buying it?   -Freshness

4. (Hold up a pen spring) Identify this object?   -Spring

5. In what season will you see these baby animals? (Hold up picture of chicks)   -Spring

6. What types of vegetables are the best in salads? -Fresh

7. (Hold up a pepper grinder) What type of ground pepper does this object give?-   -Fresh

8. If cookies just came out of the oven they are considered _____baked? -Fresh

9. What was the first scent of Downy Fabric softener?
-April Fresh

10. What is the best feature of laundry hung on a clothesline to dry? -Freshness

11. When in a car for a long time with the windows up, what do people crave? -Fresh Air

12. When people have been traveling for a long time they like to go to a Bathroom to "_____ up?" -Freshen

Objects to Sculpt (No motions, speaking or sounds allowed)	Things to Draw (No words, letters, or symbols allowed)	Songs to Hum or Kazoo (Songs must be familiar to all participants)	Things to Act Out (No speaking or sounds allowed)
-Football	-Bee on a flower	-Happy Birthday to you	-Starting a car
-Flower	-Garage Door	-The Alphabet (you will also need to accept "Twinkle, Twinkle, Little Star" and "Baa, Baa Black Sheep" for this tune)	-Giving a haircut
-Pepperoni Pizza	-Sidewalk		-Getting Ready for Bed
-Christmas Tree	-Outer Space		-Eating Spaghetti
-Pretzel	-Mud puddle		-Touchdown Play
-Skateboard	-Clown Nose		-Water Skiing
-Duck	-Camp Site	-Itsy, Bitsy Spider	-Singing into a microphone
-Dice	-Red light	-Old MacDonald	-Photographer
-Candle	-American Flag	-B-I-N-G-O	-Painting your toenails
-Teddy Bear	-Handlebars on a bike	-Jingle Bells	-Making a P,B & J sandwich
		-You Are My Sunshine	
		-The Ants Go Marching	
		-If You're Happy & You Know It	
		-Mary Had A Little Lamb	

Activity #2: Flower Arranging for Girls; Wiffle Ball for Boys

If you choose to do flower arranging at this point separate the boys and the girls. The girls will go with the "Flower Arranger" and make an arrangement to take home with them. <See Supplies List at the end of this theme chapter for details and suggestions for this activity.>

If you are not doing flower arranging then include the girls in the Wiffle ball experience.

The boys will participate in that good old spring activity of Baseball. Discuss that every spring each baseball team gets a fresh season to work with–that ties it into the theme nicely.

Discussion: Jesus Gives Us A Fresh Start!

Easter is the most important holiday that people celebrate, even though many people consider Christmas to be. Any ideas why?

Any ideas what Easter is all about?

*At Christmas we celebrate the birth of Jesus. Without Christmas there wouldn't even be an Easter. At Easter we celebrate the fact that Jesus did what He came to do for us. He died on the cross for our sins. But dying was not the only thing that Jesus did. That **was** extremely important! But Easter Sunday is not a celebration of His death–it is a celebration of the fact that, not only did Jesus die for us, but He also beat death. He became alive again, after He had died and was buried.*

Show a video/DVD that will present the resurrection story. If your group of kids can handle it show the end of the crucifixion from "The Passion of the Christ"–just before Jesus dies. Keep in mind that, while excellent in its realistic portrayal of the event it may be too graphic for your kids. Preview it ahead of time to know how much to show.

This is how it is told in the Bible, in John 20:1–18 *(The Message):*

> Early on the first day of the week, while it was still dark, Mary Magdalene went to the tomb and saw that the stone had been removed from the entrance. So she came running to Simon Peter and the other disciple, the one Jesus loved, and said, "They have

taken the Lord out of the tomb, and we don't know where they have put him!"

So Peter and the other disciple started for the tomb. Both were running, but the other disciple outran Peter and reached the tomb first. He bent over and looked in at the strips of linen lying there but did not go in. Then Simon Peter, who was behind him, arrived and went into the tomb. He saw the strips of linen lying there, as well as the burial cloth that had been around Jesus' head. The cloth was folded up by itself, separate from the linen. Finally the other disciple, who had reached the tomb first, also went inside. He saw and believed. (They still did not understand from Scripture that Jesus had to rise from the dead.)

Then the disciples went back to their homes, but Mary stood outside the tomb crying. As she wept, she bent over to look into the tomb and saw two angels in white, seated where Jesus' body had been, one at the head and the other at the foot.

They asked her, "Woman, why are you crying?"

"They have taken my Lord away," she said, "and I don't know where they have put him."

At this, she turned around and saw Jesus standing there, but she did not realize that it was Jesus.

"Woman," he said, "why are you crying? Who is it you are looking for?"

Thinking he was the gardener, she said, "Sir, if you have carried him away, tell me where you have put him, and I will get him."

Jesus said to her, "Mary."

She turned toward him and cried out in Aramaic, "Rabboni!" (Which means Teacher).

Jesus said, "Do not hold on to me, for I have not yet returned to the Father. Go instead to my brothers and tell them, 'I am returning to my Father and your Father, to my God and your God.'"

Mary Magdalene went to the disciples with the news: "I have

seen the Lord!" And she told them that he had said these things to her.

In order for Jesus to complete what He was sent by God to do for us, He had to die. His blood fulfilled the need for a sacrifice–which is what people offered to God for the fact they were not perfect in Bible times. A sacrifice had to be the best animal they had. It had to be killed and offered in a ceremonial way, to show God that they were sorry for their sins.

We don't need to offer an animal as sacrifice today because God gave us Jesus. His blood and His death are the sacrifices for our sins.

God offered Jesus in this way because He loves us. Jesus died, but, even better, He rose again to life, and lives still. That is important because it means that God has given us a way to be free of our sins and live in Heaven with God, either after our body dies or after Jesus returns for us–all because of Jesus. We are fresh and renewed by Jesus. Our sins are covered and we are given new life because of His love for us.

The only thing that is required of us is to believe that He did this for us and that there is no other way to be free of our sins than with Jesus.

That is what Easter is all about.

This is a perfect opportunity to offer an invitation to accept Jesus. You need to be ready to offer one at anytime it is appropriate, and you need to be extremely comfortable with the words you use to share it. If you have not done so already prepare, in your own words, the words for your invitation. Remember, it needs to be simple for kids to understand, sincere in its tone and succinct in its delivery. For an example of an invitation you will find one in the "Salvation Invitation" section of this book.

If anyone accepts your invitation and asks Jesus into their heart for the first time please make it a special celebration with the rest of the group. It's not a time for embarrassment but they should be aware of their awesome step of faith. Tell them that there is a party in Heaven at that moment for the place that has been reserved for them!

Closing Activity: Steal the "Fresh" item.

This is steal the bacon with items considered to be fresh.

Suggestions for items:

1. Fresh Produce–a head of lettuce perhaps, or a radish or something else
2. A can of Air Freshener
3. A slice of fresh bread
4. A fresh flower
5. A container of "Fruit Fresh"
6. Downy "April Fresh" fabric softener or dryer sheet

Supplies Needed for "Fresh" Based on Funds available			
Activity	Budget	Budget w/ some frills	Bells & Whistles
Sculpting, Drawing, Humming, Charades	-4 containers of Play-Doh -4 pencils -4 pads of paper	Same plus enough kazoos for 1 per player	Same
Flower Arranging	Do not do this activity unless you have some money to invest in the fresh flowers and greens.	-Instruct girls to bring their own vases ahead of time -Enough Fresh flowers and greens for each girl to make an arrangement. Purchase from a wholesaler to get the most for your money. -Flower cutting shears – several pairs for girls to share -Water source -Someone who knows how to do flower arranging and will teach the girls about it	-All flower arranging supplies provided -Someone that can instruct the girls on flower arranging and supervise the process – Some professionals will volunteer their time for this and you only need to pay for the supplies. Each girl should make identical arrangements so the person supervising need only teach one arrangement and they follow that example. -Water source

Wiffle Ball	-Wiffle Ball Bat -Wiffle Ball or soft foam balls -Bases	Same plus additional bats and balls for selection and a tee if necessary	Same
Discussion	-Bible -TV/VCR or DVD Player -Easter video or DVD. Consider "The Passion of the Christ" (after the graphic flogging, if you think your kids can handle it)	Same	Same
Steal the Fresh Item	-Cones -Masking tape for lines -Fresh Produce lettuce, radish, carrots -Air Freshener -A slice of fresh bread -A fresh flower -A container of "Fruit Fresh" -Downy "April Fresh" fabric softener or dryer sheet -Febreze	Same	Same

Friendship

Theme Target:
Teach kids what it means to be a true friend. Remind them of the ultimate friendship action by Jesus.

Golden Nugget:
Who's your best friend? Are you a true friend?

Scripture:
1 Samuel 20 (The Message) and Greater love has no man than this… John 15:12–14 (NIV)

Activity #1: Protect the Celebrity

This is circle dodgeball with a twist. All players stand in a circle except two. The two stand in the center. One is the Celebrity and the other is his Bodyguard. All players on the circle are throwing a ball, or more than one ball to spruce it up, attempting to hit the Celebrity. The Bodyguard is doing everything he/she can to prevent the Celebrity from being hit. The bodyguard can be hit as many times as necessary to accomplish this. If the Celebrity is hit the following transition occurs:

1. The Bodyguard joins the outer circle, in the spot that is now vacant.

2. The Celebrity becomes the new Bodyguard.

3. The hitter becomes the new Celebrity.

This is tons of fun but you will need to stop the game periodically to fix the circle as it will rapidly change shape, becoming unrecognizable as a circle and narrowing the playing area.

Every remaining activity requires the kids to be in teams of two. Instruct them to, "Choose a partner. This is an important selection and should be someone that you trust to be your partner for the rest of the event."

In the event that you have un uneven number of kids, or boys to girls, make sure you have one male and one female leader that would make a great partner to a kid.

Activity #2: 3-legged race

Give each pair something to tie their legs together with at the ankles.

This is the age-old game of tying two ankles together and coordinating steps to win a race. Either run all the pairs at the same time or break it up into heats.

Activity #3: Friendship tag (elbow tag)

Divide the group into pairs. Have partners link elbows and stand anywhere in the playing area, leaving at least ten feet between each pair. Choose one pair to start it off. One is it and trying to catch the other. If the chaser tags the runner they immediately swap roles and the original runner has to tag him back. A runner can escape being tagged (and take a rest from running) by simply running to one of the standing pairs and linking elbows with one of the pair to make a threesome.

In this game, two is company but three is a crowd! When the runner latches on, the one member of the pair whose arm was not linked with must break away at top speed. This player instantly becomes new prey for "It"—until he dashes to yet another pair for safety. The confusing transitions can provide a break for weary runners and give even a slow moving "It" a chance to catch the runner.

Always be ready to change it up yourself when "It" is struggling or if some kids aren't getting a turn to run.

Activity #4: Back-to-Back

This is the game where you start out with two people sitting back to back and they have to stand straight up without using their hands. Combine successful pairs, one pair at a time, after every successful attempt.

Activity #5: Make Friendship Bracelets

If you have a leader that knows how to make really unique and cool bracelets or a book with instructions on how to do so refer to that. Otherwise, following are simplest instructions for making friendship bracelets:

Step 1: Each kid selects three colors of embroidery floss.

Step 2: Cut 18" of each color of floss selected.

Step 3: Tie a knot with the three strands ¼"–½" from the end.

Step 4: Duct tape the knotted end to a table.

Step 5: Braid the three strands together until braid is long enough to wrap around wrist.

Step 6: Knot the strands.

Step 7: Tie around wrist to desired tightness.

Step 8: Cut off excess.

Discussion: What does it take to be a great friend?

Watch a clip from a movie in which a friend was helped out by another friend in his time of need. Suggestions: The Fox and the Hound; Toy Story (one or two); Finding Nemo (at the end, when they find Nemo and then Dory wants to remain friends with them because her life has been changed), or any movie you are partial to that exemplifies true friendship.

What is a friend?

What did the character(s) in the movie do for the friend?

What are some things that good friends do for each other?

There is a great story in the Bible about two boys that are best friends. In this story one of the boys saves the other one's life.

Ask for four volunteers—make sure two of them that you select are known to be good friends. The four volunteers will act out the story as you read it and they will play: King Saul, David, Jonathan and the servant that collects the arrows.

Determine which character each will play, giving the roles of David and Jonathan to the good friends. Give them each a headpiece to honor their role—a crown, paper or otherwise, for Saul, a towel or piece of fabric for the others with a strip of cloth tied around it to hold it on their head. For added effect the cloth should reflect their status—Jonathan is a prince so something far nicer than the servant's would be appropriate.

You will also need a safety bow and arrows. Saul will need something attached to his waist to be a spear, to be thrown at Jonathan later.

Give each character a placard to wear around their neck that has their character's name on it. The appearance of the name on it should reflect the status of the character as well—Saul's most fancy, then Jonathan's, David's and finally, the servant's being very plain and the edges torn or tattered.

Instruct the actors that they will provide the action for the story, acting out what you read. Tell the servant that his/her role is very small and does not come in until much later in the story and you will give an obvious cue for his/her presence.

Read each line slowly and with great expression and emphasis. Allow your actors time to act out what you are saying.>

Okay, this story takes place in 1 Samuel, chapter twenty.

David and Jonathan were friends.

They were good friends.

They were best friends.

(If necessary) They were much better friends than that!

Jonathan was the son of the King. (Point to Saul)

King Saul was a very powerful King.

He was rich—as most Kings are.

He was greedy.

He was not a good king at all.

King Saul knew God was going to make David the next King, instead of his son Jonathan.

Saul did not like David.

He actually hated David!

He wanted David dead!

David sensed that Saul wanted to kill him.

He asked Jonathan if it was true.

Jonathan didn't know anything about it and didn't believe that his father would kill David. His Dad knew David was his best friend and he thought his Dad would never harm him.

David was concerned. He asked Jonathan about it.

He said to him,

> "What do I do now? What wrong have I inflicted on your father that makes him so determined to kill me?"

> "Nothing," said Jonathan. "You've done nothing wrong.

> And you're not going to die.

> Really, you're not!

> My father tells me everything. He does nothing, whether big or little, without confiding in me. So why would he do this behind my back? It can't be."

But David said, "Your father knows that we are the best of friends. So he says to himself, 'Jonathan must know nothing of this. If he does, he'll side with David.' But it's true—as sure as God lives, and as sure as you're alive before me right now—he's determined to kill me."

Jonathan said, "Tell me what you have in mind. I'll do anything for you."

David had a plan to find out whether the King wanted him dead or not.

David said, "Tomorrow marks the New Moon. I'm scheduled to eat dinner with the king.

Instead, I'll go hide in the field…

If your father misses me, say to him, 'David asked if he could run down to Bethlehem, his hometown, for an anniversary reunion, and worship with his family.'

If he responds to that by saying, 'Good!' then I'm safe.

But if he gets angry, you'll know for sure that he's made up his mind to kill me.

Please stick with me in this. If I have wronged him and he plans to kill me, go ahead and kill me yourself. Why bother giving me up to your father?"

"Never!" exclaimed Jonathan. "I'd never do that!

If I get the slightest hint that my father wants to kill you, I'll tell you."

David asked, "And how exactly will you let me know that is what he wants to do?"

—Jonathan thought for a minute.

No, he really thought hard.

Harder.

Then, he came up with a plan.

"Come outside," said Jonathan. "Let's go to the field."

When the two of them were out in the field, Jonathan said, "As God, the God of Israel, is my witness, by this time tomorrow I'll get it out of my father how he feels about you.

Then I'll let you know what I learn. May God do his worst to me if I let you down!

If my father intends to kill you, I'll tell you and get you out of here in one piece."

Jonathan then laid out his plan:
They huddled together and Jonathan gave him all the details.

"Tomorrow is the New Moon, and you'll be missed when you don't show up for dinner. On the third day, when they've quit expecting you, come to the place where you hid before, and wait beside that big boulder. I'll shoot three arrows in the direction of the boulder. Then I'll send off my servant, 'Go find the arrows.'

If I yell after the servant, 'The arrows are on this side! Retrieve them!' that's the signal that you can return safely—not a thing to fear!

But if I yell, 'The arrows are farther out!' then run for it—God wants you out of here!

Regarding all the things we've discussed, remember that God's in on this with us to the very end!"

They agreed on the plan and went ahead with it.
David hid in the field.

On the holiday of the New Moon, the king came to the table to eat. He sat where he always sat, the place against the wall, with Jonathan across the table. David's seat was empty.

Saul didn't mention it at the time, thinking, "Something's happened that's made him unclean. That's it—he's probably unclean for the holy meal."

But the day after the New Moon, day two of the holiday, David's seat was still empty. Saul asked Jonathan about it,

"So where's David? He hasn't eaten with us either yesterday or today."

Jonathan said, "David asked my special permission to go to Bethlehem. He said, 'Allow me to attend a family reunion back home. My brothers have ordered me to be there. If it seems all right to you, let me go and see my brothers.'

That's why he's not here at the king's table."

Saul exploded in anger at Jonathan: "You blank-ety-blank-blank!

Don't you think I know that you're in cahoots with David? You are a disgrace! For as long as David is alive, your future in this kingdom is at risk. He will be the next King, not you, as it should be. Now go get him. Bring him here. From this moment, he's as good as dead!"

Jonathan stood up to his father. "Why dead? What's he done?"

Saul threw his spear at him to kill him. That convinced Jonathan that his father was determined to kill David.

Jonathan stormed from the table, furiously angry, and ate nothing the rest of the day, upset for David and hurt from the humiliation from his father.

(Have a leader give Jonathan his bow and arrows.)

In the morning, Jonathan went to the field for the appointment with David.

He had his young servant with him.

Now is when he had his young servant with him.

(If the servant doesn't get his/her cue) **Servant—with him—now.**

He told the servant, "Run and get the arrows I'm about to shoot."

The boy started running and Jonathan shot an arrow way beyond him.

As the boy came to the area where the arrow had been shot, Jonathan yelled out, "Isn't the arrow farther out?"

He yelled again, "Hurry! Quickly! Don't just stand there!"

Though he was confused, Jonathan's servant then picked up the arrow and brought it to his master.

The boy, of course, knew nothing of what was going on. Only Jonathan and David knew.

Jonathan gave his bow and arrows to the boy and sent him back to town.

After the servant was gone, David got up from his hiding place beside the boulder, then fell on his face to the ground! And then they said goodbye to each other and cried.

David cried especially hard.

Harder.

Way harder than that!

Jonathan said, "Go in peace!

-The end-

Thank your actors and allow them to take their bows.

Jonathan risked his own life to save David's. His father was so mad that he would have killed his own son to get rid of David. Jonathan loved David so much that he was willing to die for him.

There is another person in the Bible that actually did give up His life for His friends. That person is Jesus. He was sent to the earth by God to die for everyone else.

In John 15: 12–14 (NIV) Jesus said this:

My command is this: Love each other as I have loved you. Greater love has no one than this, that he lay down his life for his friends. You are my friends if you do what I command.

Are you His friend? Did He die for you? Do you believe that Jesus died for you, to save you from your sins?

If it feels right this is a perfect opportunity to offer an invitation to accept Jesus. You need to be ready to offer one at anytime it is appropriate, and you need to be extremely comfortable with the words you use to share it. If you have not done so already prepare, in your own words, the words for your invitation. Remember, it needs to be simple for kids to understand, sincere in its tone and succinct in its delivery. For an example of an invitation you will find one in the "Salvation Invitation" section of this book.

If anyone accepts your invitation and asks Jesus into their heart for the first time please make it a special celebration with the rest of the group. It's not a time for embarrassment but they should be aware of their awesome step of faith. Tell them that there is a party in Heaven at that moment for the place that has been reserved for them!

Closing Activity: Marshmallow Pitch

Put down two masking tape lines, running parallel. The lines should be long enough that all pairs can line up—one partner on each side, facing each other–with several feet separating them from the next pair.

Give each pair a cup full of mini marshmallows–or another small, edible item that can be tossed easily and caught in the mouth without hurting teeth or traveling down the throat too quickly and causing choking (how many of us have nearly choked on an M & M that went right down our throat without touching our tongue, or nearly chipped a tooth when misjudged?)–other suggestions are Cap 'N Crunch or Cheerios cereal.

One kid is the mini marshmallow pitcher; the other is the mini marshmallow catcher. The catcher gets down on their knees and awaits the pitch.

The pitcher takes one mini marshmallow at a time and pitches it to the catcher, whose goal is to catch the marshmallow in his/her mouth.

Supplies Needed for "Friendship" Based on Funds available			
Activity	Budget	Budget w/ some frills	Bells & Whistles
Protect the Celebrity	-Balls that don't hurt when hit in the face	Same	Same
3-Legged Race	-Cones for end lines -Masking tape for end lines -Strips of rope or cloth to tie legs together	Same	Same
Elbow Tag	Nothing	Nothing	Nothing
Back to Back	Nothing	Nothing	Nothing
Make Friendship Bracelets	-Embroidery Floss (lots) -Scissors – many pairs -Duct tape	Same	Same
Discussion	-TV&VCR or DVD player -Video or DVD with scene of great friendship -Bible -Crown for Saul -Cloth and ties for headpieces -A spear for Saul -Safe bow and arrows	Same	Same
Marshmallow Pitch	-Masking tape for lines -Cups -Mini Marshmallows, Cheerios, Cap'N Crunch or other small edible items that can be tossed and caught in mouth without choking or hurting teeth	Same	Same

Glow in the Dark

Theme Target:
Teach the kids that God has given each one a special gift and is pleased when it is used for Him.

Golden Nugget:
How can you glow in a dark world?

Scripture:
Matthew 5:16 (NIV)

This is one of those events that you should save for when space is extremely limited and the kids aren't able to be as active as usual.

This event requires darkness so it is either a nighttime activity or you will need to cover the windows (and any other constant light source) in the room that you use for the "Glow-in-the-Dark" games with either heavy duty black plastic or thick black fabric, or something else that blocks out the light entirely.

This is also a great event for those "Halloween Alternatives." The kids will like it because of the "Wow" factor with the black-light effect and that is also the time of year you can find the candy items needed for the first Activity.

Preparation for the event requires you to set up a few black-lights in your darkened room–how many depends on the size of your room and how dark you can get it, the darker the better. If you don't already have these they can be purchased at Wal-Mart and they are not terribly expensive. They come in different sizes. You should only get lights that are at least 24" long. Don't just get normal light bulbs that are black-light, they need to be the fluorescent tubes. They are more intense, will activate a larger area and they don't burn as hot.

If you want to justify the purchase you should know that as soon as you use them once and see the reaction of the kids, you will look for other opportunities to work them into future events.

In darkening your room be aware that the floor can be a factor as well. If you are in a carpeted room that will be ideal, as long as the carpet is not light in color. A room with a shiny floor can actually reflect the black-light and make it too bright in the room. You will still get a cool effect but it will make some of the games too easy–still fun and the kids will still love it but you may feel a bit of disappointment in the effect.

A 20' x 20' room would probably only need four black-lights–either one on each wall (if you can get it up high so it can shine down on the room that is ideal) or two on opposing walls. Try them in different positions on the floor first, angled upward, to see what configuration gives you the best effect.

For the effect, anything that is dark in color will absorb the black-light and anything that is fluorescent or considered to be "glow-in-the-dark" will stand out in an amazing way. One thing to be aware of, light colored clothing will also be affected. A warning for the women–if you wear a black, knit sweater, or something similar to that, and you also wear white undergarments–your undergarments will show through bright and bold for everyone to see.

Don't allow any kids into your black-light room until you are ready for your first activity. The suspense may be too much for them to handle but that is the fun of it.

Activity #1: Treasure Hunt

In preparing for the event you will also prepare for this first activity. Around Halloween time you can find individually wrapped, "Glow-in-the-dark" candy. The candy itself doesn't glow but the wrappers do. These come in many varieties so choose the one that is best for you. Tip: If you do this event just after Halloween you will get the candy at a great discount.

If you don't find them or you are choosing to do this at a different time of the year there is just a bit more prep for you. Purchase individually wrapped candy, or another treat that you prefer, and make the wrapper glow in some way. This could be as elaborate as painting a symbol on it in fluorescent paint or as simple as putting a fluorescent sticker on it. Before going to a lot of trouble though make sure that what you intend to do will actually glow in the black-light by holding it close to the light source.

In your activity room "hide" the treasures. Depending on how dark it is they can be in plain sight but only the glow-in-the-dark part will show. Tape them to the wall, the ceiling (if not ridiculously high), pretty much anywhere. The kids will need to be resourceful in getting them off the ceiling, but trust me–they will. Be prepared to nix any plans that will surely result in injury.

Separate the kids into two teams–you will keep these for the entire event. While outside the activity room explain the game to them, then walk them into the room, with all the lights off–including the black-light. On "Go" you will turn on the black-lights and the game will begin.

Every kid will collect as many "treasures" as he can and put them in his team's glow-in-the-dark bucket. Once all are collected the teams count them. The team that has the most gets two of the candy items per kid. The team that lost only gets one. You keep all the others for a different event or for yourself if you are a candy freak–and you know some of you are. (You can obviously work this as you choose).

Note: If using actual "Glow-in-the-dark" items vs. fluorescent be sure to turn off your light source well in advance of this activity. Glow-in-the-dark will maintain its activation for a little while and you don't want them to see what is going on right away. If this can't be avoided or turning on all the lights at the same time is not an option, then they can begin the game as soon as you open the doors. Put smaller kids in the front so they have a better chance.

For the next activity time you will have one team play a game and the other team get creative. A leader in the creative activity should be responsible to notify the game leader when they are about ready to switch.

Activity #2: Seat of Your Pants Nuke 'Em

In your black-light room have two leaders holding up a net for this game–if you don't have a way of making it stand freely. The net can be as simple as a clothesline rope with a few fluorescent items hanging from it with clothespins so they can see what they need to throw the ball over. This does not need to be elaborate, however, if you have the means, be creative. Simple white t-shirts will glow in black-light so they could easily be used if you have nothing else that will react.

Separate the kids into two teams–one team on either side of the "net."

Have the players on each team spread out and sit on the floor. They will now play "Nuke 'Em." If you have never heard of this it is really simple volleyball–instead of hitting it over the net they should catch the ball and throw it over the net. They can still use teamwork and toss the ball to each other before throwing over the net but, in the interest of time, only allow one toss before sending it over. This also prevents buddies from just playing together.

One point is scored for the opposite team each time the ball touches the ground. Use your own judgment on whether to charge points for the kid that is messing around and wants to play by themselves by bouncing the ball on the floor a few times or anything else like that.

Also, their buttocks must remain on the floor at all times. If they rise to catch the ball and it comes off the floor charge a point.

Periodically, instruct them to find a new location on their side of the court. Some will try to move only a few inches, or return to a previous location. Insist that they find a location they have not been in before.

Tip: Establish pre-determined rotation locations. The first time they sit down give each player a piece of masking tape and have them tape it to the floor. You now have the official locations for the duration of the game, including for the next group that comes to play. (You can find fluorescent orange tape for this purpose).

Activity #3: Use Your Creative Gifts, a.k.a. Glow-in-the-Dark Artist

This activity should take place in a separate area from the black-light room. There should be table and chairs enough for everyone to sit and do their project, which is one of two things.

Have the kids make a picture of a gift that God has given them that they can use for Him. Be prepared to offer suggestions of gifts in case they don't know what you are talking about:

1. Helping others–chores, finding things, etc.

2. Encouragement (this could be through notes, verbalization, playing music, even humor)

3. Teaching others

4. Caring for younger kids (brothers and sisters, neighbors)

5. Giving to those in need

6. Prayer

Project Options

Simple and pretty cool:

Make pictures using Crayola's "Color Explosion" paper and markers. If you have not experienced this it is really cool. It is similar to the scratch pads that have colors hidden under a black, waxy covering. The picture is made by scratching away the covering to reveal the colors.

"Color Explosion" is the same concept but without the mess and possibility of scratching through the paper–or having areas scratched accidentally. With this the colors are hidden under a black surface as well but a special marker, which comes with it, is used to draw on the black. The "ink" in the marker dissolves the black and the colors appear. Some of the colors underneath may even react to black-light.

The drawback to this is that each set of paper and markers comes with only a few markers so you will need to purchase many packs of these in order to allow all kids to participate at the same time.

More elaborate but extremely cool:

Make paintings using fluorescent or glow-in-the-dark paint. If you do this one you will either need to warn the kids ahead of time to wear old clothes or use washable paint.

This is pretty self-explanatory so no need for a lot of detail. Still, there are a few suggestions to add a little "wow" to it.

If you use black paper to paint on then only what they paint will glow–pretty cool effect.

If you don't have enough brushes already you can purchase cheap ones. You will still need a water source to rinse the brush between colors so they don't get all mixed up. If you would rather not bother with that you can provide each kid one Q-tip per color of paint, to use as his or her brush.

Discussion: How can you glow in a dark world?

Take a look at the art projects. Be sure to look at every one of them. Make positive comments about them–ask them what gift they are using if they don't offer it. Pick out a few that are worthwhile to share with the entire group. If kids are willing have them explain the gift they are using in the picture.

Isn't it cool that God has given each of us gifts?

Sometimes we don't think we have a gift that we can use. Maybe you don't know what your gifts are yet. Be patient–you have a gift. God made each of us special and gave everyone gifts to be used for Him.

Sometimes we don't know how to use our gifts. Praying to God for the ability to see how to use them is necessary. Sometimes God tells you how to use your gifts and sometimes He shows other people how you can use them. It is up to you to listen and use your gifts wisely.

Sometimes we see other people's gifts and wish we had them. But we can't choose our gifts. We have no control over what God gives us, but we need to be happy with our gifts and decide how to use them in the best ways.

When we use our gifts for God His love shines through us. That is how we can glow in a very dark world. This world needs Jesus' love and it is up to us that know and love Him to bring it to the world.

Jesus tells us, in Matthew 5: 14–16 (NIV)

"You are the light of the world. A city on a hill cannot be hidden. Neither do people light a lamp and put it under a bowl. Instead they put it on its stand, and it gives light to everyone in the house. In the same way, let your light shine before men, that they may see your good deeds and praise your Father in heaven."

Will you glow in this dark world or will you blend into the darkness? You can use your gifts to praise God or you can keep them to yourself, or worse, use them to make only yourself happy. Only you can make the choice!

Closing Activity: Glow-in-the-Dark Bowling

In your black-light room set up fluorescent cones or cups in bowling fashion, one set-up per team. Place a masking tape line on the floor that they cannot cross when they bowl. Each team has one bowler at a time bowl a "frame." Both bowlers should bowl at the same time. They get two attempts to knock down all the "pins." The team with the bowler that knocks the most "pins" down in each frame earns one point for their team.

Supplies Needed for "Glow In The Dark" Based on Funds			
Activity	Budget	Budget w/ some frills	Bells & Whistles
General	-Black-lights w/ fluorescent tube bulbs -Extension cords -Something to hang black-lights with -Black construction plastic or black fabric to darken room. The darker the better. -Surge protectors – to allow one switch to turn on/off as many lights as possible.	Same	Same but with more lights

Treasure Hunt	-Individually wrapped candy, or other treat, that reacts to black-light -Fluorescent basket, box or bucket. -Fluorescent stickers or paint to make candy wrappers glow if necessary	Same	Same
Seat of Your Pants Nuke 'Em	-Fluorescent Masking tape -Clothesline or rope -Clothespins -Black-light reactive items to hang from clothesline -Ball that glows fluorescent – either paint a ball, use a ball with a glow stick in it or use a ball that is glow-in-the-dark ("Gertie" balls come in some glow-in-the-dark colors.)	Same but with a Gertie Ball – can be purchased at toy stores, is only a few dollars and is easy to inflate and deflate and is a great dodgeball ball as well	Same as Budget but with a freestanding volleyball or badminton net lined with fluorescent tape.
Glow-in-the-Dark Artist	-Newspaper or plastic to cover tables -Paper -Glow-in-the-dark paint (can be purchased at Wal-Mart or craft-stores) in pint cans or larger. -Paint brushes or Q-tips – if using this paint only 1 Q-tip is needed since there is only 1 color -Paper plates, bowls or aluminum pie tins to put paint in	Same as Budget but with different colors of Fluorescent paint and 1 Q-tip per color for each kid Or -Color Explosion supplies	Same as Budget with frills
Discussion	-Bible	Same	Same
Glow-in-the-Dark Bowling	-Fluorescent cones or cups, or something else to serve as "pins" -2 Balls that react to black-light "Gertie" Balls recommended as they are a great addition to your general supplies.	Same	Same

Gross

Theme Target:
God created the earth and all its living creatures. He created man and all of his bodily functions. In all of His creation everything was good—even some things that we think are gross!

Golden Nugget:
Sin is the grossest thing in the world to God!

Scripture:
Multiple passages about gross things.

There are a number of activities suggested here. To do all of them would require several hours of time. Either use this for a lengthier event or pick and choose your favorites.

Activity #1: Name that Jelly Bean

For this activity you will need to purchase a pack or two of "Bertie Bott's" from Jelly Belly. They are actual Jelly Belly jellybeans but they are in the worst flavors imaginable. They come in a pack of assorted flavors. Yes, they are expensive for jellybeans, especially if you need to have them shipped (call a candy store that carries jelly bellies and see if they carry them–some do).

If you choose to do this activity don't improvise–get the actual Bertie Bott's. They look like normal jellybeans but just wait till you see the kid's faces! It is worth it for the fun you will have watching this one.

First things first–you **must** try all of the Bertie Bott's Jelly Bellies. You need to do this to decide if you need to take any out of the selection. Periodically they introduce new flavors and remove others but they had a vomit flavor and it definitely lived up to its name!

Separate the Bertie Bott's into the Dixie cups by flavor. Number each cup.

For the game distribute the "Guess Sheets." Each player is on his or her own for this one. They get one of each flavor and must decide what flavor it is. Tell them that they are "Jelly Bellies" and that Jelly Belly is famous for having a lot of unique flavors.–Be sure to open your event with this game so they don't realize that the theme is "Gross" and you are setting them up for the reaction you are sure to get.

After everyone is done guessing see who got the most right. Award a prize of mouthwash or mints to the winner.

Separate the kids into two teams for the remainder of this event.

Jelly Bean Guess Sheet

Sample #	Guess
1	
2	
3	
4	
5	
6	
7	
8	
9	
10	

Jelly Bean Guess Sheet

Sample #	Guess
1	
2	
3	
4	
5	
6	
7	
8	
9	
10	

Activity #2: Steal the gross item

This is "Steal the Bacon" but they are stealing gross items like: Baby diaper with melted candy bar in it; Sardines or other fish–if you have an ethnic food store near you get something from the fish department there; Fake dog vomit–melt a few caramels, place a few nuggets of dog food in it while melted, let harden—you will be amazed how gross this looks!; Snotty tissue—No, Not a real one!—you need jello for the next game… make a batch of lemon jello, while it is still liquid dip a tissue into it… this will look very authentic!

Players may not toss the item over their line it must be carried. If tagged while holding the item they must drop it where it is and go back to their own line and tag a teammate before returning to "steal" the item.

Don't hesitate to put more than one item out at a time and call multiple numbers–or not.

Activity #3: Jello slurp

Before your event make a few batches of jello–set it in muffin cups. Once set put one muffin cup of jello into the foot of a knee-high for every contestant you will have. Keep these refrigerated until ready for the game.

Give each kid a jello knee-high. On "Go" they will eat the jello–through the foot of the knee-high as quickly as possible. The first team that has every kid finish their jello wins the game.

Activity #4: Candy sculpture

Each team should select a leader or two (these need to be brave souls). Don't inform them, but the leader is the "sculptor"–if a team selects a leader that will not be a good sport about this project you should select a new one for them.

Give each team leader, or set of leaders, a sculpting surface and a bowl. Give the rest of the team a supply of chewy candy and a trash bag. They are the "laborers."

On "GO" the "laborers" will begin unwrapping their candy and chewing it until pliable. They cannot eat the candy–they only chew it long enough to sculpt with. When it is pliable they put it into the bowl by their sculptor.

The sculptor is to make a sculpture using only the candy that has been deposited into the bowl.

When you announce that time is up all candy in chewing process is to be chewed and swallowed and the sculpting must cease. Allow sculptors to get cleaned up and move sculptures to judging area.

Judges will award points for:

1. Creativity

2. Use of color

3. Height

4. Stability

5. Effort

6. Sportsmanship

7. Artistic impression

Share judges awards at end of event.

Activity #5: Popeye Relay

Set up cones and masking tape fault line at beginning point of relay. One at a time each contestant will run down to the table and scoop one mouthful of spinach out of their team's bowl and transfer it to the weigh-in container. They cannot use their hands for anything.

Once deposited in the container they run back to their line. Once they cross the line the next player may go.

The team that has transferred the most weight in spinach and is sitting quietly wins the game.

Activity #6: Burping Contest

Each team, without knowing the task, should select one or more representatives. You decide how many contestants you want to allow for this one. The representatives come to the front of the group. You will hand each one a can of soda. On "Go" they must drink the entire can of soda.

Flip a coin to see which team goes first.

One at a time the representatives will attempt to perform the grossest burp.

You will need a few leaders to act as impartial judges. Give them Scorecards and have them hold up their score immediately and have a scorekeeper calculate the totals. Or–give them score sheets and they can award points for the following categories:

1. Volume

2. Duration

3. Creativity–do they speak as they burp or can they burp their name or alphabet?

4. Gross–Factor–was it juicy?

Give each contestant a prize–An antacid tablet would be appropriate!

Activity #7: The Milky Way

Attach a rubber glove to the bottom of a sawhorse for each team, so it hangs down like an udder. Poke a hole or two in the tip of each finger. Pour equal amounts of milk into each glove–for more fun use chocolate milk.

One by one each contestant will be allowed thirty seconds to milk the cow. The pail is, yup—you guessed it, the mouth of a teammate. Either assign one "pail" for the entire game, or, the milker becomes the pail at the end of his thirty seconds. The first "pail" would then be the last milker.

Either the first team to drain their utter or the team with the least spillage, wins the game. You could also do both. If you want to offer a prize you could give one milk dud to each player.

Discussion: What is gross to God!

What is the grossest thing you can possibly think of?

Did you know that the Bible is filled with all kinds of things that we would consider gross?

Share a few gross facts:

- God sent his people food everyday as they walked around in the desert. It was called Manna. Each morning He gave them enough for that day. Some people got greedy and didn't trust they would have enough the next day so they would try to hide it and save it. What they would find the next day is that it had rotted and was full of maggots and stank really bad! (Exodus 16:19–24 NIV)

- There was a king in the Bible that was really, really fat. He was so fat that when he was attacked by a man that tried to kill him, the guy stabbed him in the belly with a sword that was one & ½ feet long (demonstrate the length with your hands) - and he lost the sword in his belly! (Judges 3:16–22 NIV)

- A great big fish swallowed Jonah and he stayed in his stomach for three days until the fish spit him out. Major indigestion!! What do you think it smelled like on the inside of a fish belly?

- John the Baptist ate locusts (bugs bigger and crunchier than grasshoppers) with wild honey (Matthew 3:4 NIV)–he may have had to fight the bees for the honey!

- Peter was told by God, in a vision, that he should kill and eat all kinds of four-footed animals, as well as reptiles of the earth and birds of the air–maybe lizards and bugs?

Characters were always having visions of gross creatures:

God told Job about a huge fire-breathing swamp dragon called Leviathan (Job 41 NIV)

Ezekiel had one with four creatures and each had four faces–a lion, an ox, a man and an eagle (Ezekiel 1:5–10 NIV). They each had four wings too.

Ezekiel also had a vision of dry old bones coming back to life and form-

ing skeletons, and then muscles and skin—to create an army of zombies (Ezekiel 37:1–10 NIV)

An enormous red dragon with seven heads and ten horns (Rev. 12:3 NIV)

-The Bible talks about vomit thirteen times. One time it even mentions a dog vomiting and then returning to it to eat it again (2 Peter 2:22 NIV).

-The Bible mentions blood a lot - you could read about it for a long time. In 1 Kings 22:37–38 it talks about dogs licking up the blood of a dead king. THAT IS REALLY GROSS!!

-One bad king was eaten alive by worms! (Acts 12:23 NIV)

That's a lot of pretty gross stuff in the Bible isn't it? There are lots more too—you can find it all throughout the Bible.

With all that gross stuff what do you think is the worst?

God created every creature—even the gross ones. He also made a lot of the gross things that are in the Bible happen. Do you think God thinks of those things as gross? (-can there be a right or wrong answer here?)

With all the gross stuff in the Bible and in the world what do you think is the grossest thing to God?

SIN!!

Our sin is the grossest possible thing in God's eyes. He loves us so much, but He does not love our sin. That's why He gave His son Jesus. Without Jesus we are just gross. With Jesus we are beautiful!

When you sin, imagine how God feels about it. Hopefully it makes you sorry that you sinned. Fortunately, if you have accepted Jesus, being sorry and telling God you're sorry is all that is necessary to get rid of the gross and be beautiful again.

This may be an opportunity to offer an invitation to accept Jesus. You need to be ready to offer one at anytime it is appropriate, and you need to be extremely comfortable with the words you use to share it. If you have not done so already prepare, in your own words, the words for your invitation. Remember, it needs to be simple for kids to understand, sincere in

its tone and succinct in its delivery. For an example of an invitation you will find one in the "Salvation Invitation" section of this book.

If anyone accepts your invitation and asks Jesus into their heart for the first time please make it a special celebration with the rest of the group. It's not a time for embarrassment but they should be aware of their awesome step of faith. Tell them that there is a party in Heaven at that moment for the place that has been reserved for them!

Activity #8: Goldfish Transfer

This is a relay race.

One by one each team member will run down to the table and transfer the live goldfish from its container of water into the empty container of water with their bare hands. The smaller the fish the harder it is to catch it and transfer it. Note: Be sure you have a good home for the goldfish after this event.

The first team to have each member make a successful transfer wins the game.

Closing Activity: Chubby Bunny

Each team should select one or more representative for this game—you decide how many each team should allow.

Each contestant should come up to the front of the group. You will hand them each a slip of paper that says: "*The grossest thing in God's eyes is sin.*"

Have them each read the saying aloud.

Give each contestant a Marshmallow or Brussels sprout. The contestants each put the Marshmallow or Brussels sprout in their mouth. Contestants may not chew the Marshmallows or Brussels sprouts or swallow them.

They each read the saying aloud again. If able to say it understandably they continue to the next round where they add another Marshmallow or Brussels sprout.

Any time a player cannot fit any more in their mouth and read the saying understandably they are eliminated and may spit the contents of their mouth into the trashcan. The player with the most in their mouth and can still be understood–wins the game. Award them a prize for their efforts–perhaps a toothbrush and toothpaste.

Supplies Needed for "Gross" Based on Funds available			
Activity	Budget	Budget w/ some frills	Bells & Whistles
Name that Jelly Bean	-Dixie Cups -Jelly Belly "Bertie Bott's" -Pencils -Guess sheets	Same	Same

Steal the gross item	-Cones
	
	-Masking tape for lines
	
	-Gross items to steal
	
	Suggestions:
	
	   Baby diaper with melted candy bar in it;
	
	   Sardines or other fish–if you have an ethnic food store near you get something from the fish department there;
	
	   Fake dog vomit–melt a few caramels, place a few nuggets of dog food in it while melted, let harden
	
	   Snotty tissue—make a batch of lemon jello, while it is still liquid dip a tissue into it… this will look very authentic!
		Same	Same

Jello slurp	-1 pair of knee-high stockings for every 2 kids -Jello	Same	Same
Candy sculpture	-Lots of chewy candy – a variety is good -- tootsie rolls, starburst, bubble gum, gummy bears, caramels -Cutting board or disposable plate (something to make the sculpture on) -2 bowls -2 trash bags	Same	Same

Popeye Relay	-2 large bowls of cooked spinach -2 large, empty bowls or buckets -2 digital scales -Table -Masking tape for lines	Same	Same
Burping Contest	-1 8 ounce can or cup of soda per contestant – Coke or Root Beer is suggested	Same	Same
Goldfish Transfer	-2 live goldfish -4 goldfish bowls or clear plastic containers -Table -Masking tape for lines	Same	Same
Discussion	-Bible -Gross Facts	Same	Same
The Milky Way	-1 pair Rubber gloves -2 sawhorses -Milk or chocolate milk -Disposable drop cloth -Towels for clean-up	Same	Same
Chubby Bunny	-Marshmallows or Brussels sprouts -Trash can with liner in it -Cards with saying to read on them	Same	Same
General	Prizes for any game you see worthy.	Same	Same

Impossible

Theme Target:
Teach kids about the miracles of Jesus.

Golden Nugget:
Nothing is impossible with God.

Scripture:
Miracles of Jesus

In this theme you get to have a blast getting kids to think you have some tricks up your sleeve–which you do. You will need to milk this for all its worth by getting the kids to attempt to do some of the activities, or experiments, while you withhold the critical piece of information from them that will achieve the unbelievable.

Activity #1: Impossible Stand

Separate the kids into groups of eight to ten. Provide one 16" x 16" platform for each group. On "Go" they must all stand on the platform together and hold it for twenty seconds–no feet can touch the floor during that twenty seconds. The first team to figure out how to do it gets a prize. Provide a piece of candy for each member of the team that completes the task.

They will try but most likely be unsuccessful. Don't let them give up too quickly. Tell them to be creative.

The solution: Each kid puts enough of one foot on the platform to provide stability. They then reach one hand across the platform to a person on the other side and firmly grasp. Pulling each other will provide enough resistance to hold each other up and they can lift the other foot off the ground. They work together to counterbalance their weight so match up kids similar in size when you show the solution.

You may need to adjust the size of the platform based on the size of their feet.

They will be amazed that it works.

Activity #2: Impossible Volleyball

Separate into two teams.

You will play volleyball according to normal volleyball rules, but use a balloon as the ball. Use a heavier weight balloon like a punch ball, or at least a sixteen-inch balloon. Before inflating the balloon put a weighted object in it–like a coin or marble or something like that. The object will cause the balloon to change direction as it shifts in the flight of the balloon.

For an added twist, or if you have a lot of kids, insist that they not move from a fixed location–give a piece of masking tape at beginning of game when they first get into position; instruct them to put the tape on the floor. From that point on, the occupant of that position must keep one foot on the tape at all times.

Activity #3: Impossible Experiments

Poke or Pop

Whatcha' need:

* One balloon
* A Kebab stick
* Vaseline

Whatcha' do:

* Blow up the balloon until it's about as big as your head.
* Put Vaseline on half of the Kebab stick–it needs to be as slippery as possible
* Push the Kebab stick slowly through the balloon.

Whatcha' think? Impossible? Maybe, maybe not.

Straw through a potato

Whatcha' need:

* Plastic straw
* Raw potato

Whatcha' Do:

* You are going to stab the straw through the potato without bending or breaking the straw.

How?

Hold the potato tightly, with your fingers on the front and thumb on the back—not on the top and bottom.

With the straw in your strong hand cap the top end with your thumb—that is the secret. Hold on firmly to both the straw and the potato and with a quick, sharp stab, drive the straw into and partway out of the narrow end of the spud and not the fatter middle part.

Whatcha' Think?

Alright, alright—you're so cool! Enough already!

The kids will be amazed and want to try it. Let them if you have enough supplies and time. You decide whether you tell them the secret or leave them thinking you are unbelievable!

Windbag

Whatcha' Need:

A long, tube shaped bag, open on both ends.

You can purchase "Windbags" from toy stores that sell science experiments; you can make your own long bag using a product called a Diaper Genie refill. It's part of a diaper system that parents use to store diapers. A Diaper Genie refill is commonly available at grocery stores or other stores with baby items.

Whatcha' Do:

If using the Diaper Genie Refill, cut eight-foot long tubes, as many as you want.

There are actually two amazing challenges with this simple item:

The first one: Separate the kids into groups and give each group a bag. Instruct them to tie a knot in one end. Then tell them to count how many breaths it takes to blow it up but hold it closed, do not tie a knot in the 2nd end. Depending on the size of the person, it may take anywhere from ten to fifty breaths of air.

When all teams are done have them report the number of breaths.

Now you can really impress them. Tell them that you can do it in one breath! Really–you can.

Tie a knot in your bag.

Ask someone to hold up the knotted end at eye level.

Stretch out the bag. Hold the open end of the bag about six-eight inches away from your mouth.

Blow as hard as you can into the bag. Remember to keep your mouth away from it when you blow.

Quickly seal the bag with your hand so that none of the air escapes.

The kids will think you have a different kind of bag than theirs.

Now for the second challenge—this will amaze everyone.

Use your "Windbag" to lift a table with a kid on it.

Lay as many deflated "windbags" as you have or want to use across a table so both ends hang over the edges. Tie a knot in one end of each windbag–if you haven't already done this.

Invert another table on top of the windbags, so the legs are on top.

Have one or more kids sit on the tables.

Have one kid blow into each windbag and watch the bags inflate and the table rise, even with the kids sitting on them.

Whatcha' Think?

Awesome, isn't it?

Blow up a balloon with vinegar and baking soda

★ Prepare this experiment before the event and bring it, ready to go.

★ Put ½ cup clear vinegar in a colored soda or water bottle.

★ Using a funnel put three tablespoons baking soda inside a nine-inch colored balloon.

★ Attach the balloon to the top of the bottle and let it hang off with the baking soda at the bottom.

★ Prep work is done!

When ready for this experiment simply state that you can blow up the balloon while it is still attached to the bottle.

Whatcha' Do:

Raise the bottom of the balloon and let the baking soda drop into the vinegar and watch as it goes to work blowing up the balloon.

**Try this ahead of time and make any adjustments to amounts of ingredients to ensure the balloon will inflate but prevent the reaction from being too strong and spill over.

Whatcha' Think?

Hopefully they didn't see the baking soda fall into the bottle. If they did, no big deal, they can't think you're not trying to trick them by now anyway.

Negative inflation

Whatcha' Need:

- ✶ 16 oz. plastic soda bottle
- ✶ Hot water
- ✶ 1 Bowl
- ✶ 1 pitcher or a sink
- ✶ Cold water
- ✶ Balloon

Whatcha' Do:

Fill a plastic soda bottle with hot water—*NOT boiling water*—and fill a bowl with cold water.

Let them sit for one minute.

After one minute empty the bottle quickly into the pitcher or sink.

Quickly stretch the opening of the balloon over the open end of the bottle and push the bottle down into the cold water.

Whatcha' Think?

Discussion: Jesus can do impossible things.

If you have access to a video or DVD of Jesus performing miracles have the kids watch as much as you have time for.

Jesus, the Son of God, could do anything. He had all of God's power. People couldn't believe the things that He did.

The Bible has stories of all of the unbelievable things that He did. They are called miracles. Following are some of the miracles He performed.

(Read as many as you would like and offer brief explanations for them if necessary)

Miracles in Nature:

Calmed the storm
Fed 5000 people with 5 loaves of bread and 2 fish
Walked on water
Overflowed the fish nets
He caused a coin for taxes to appear in a fish's mouth
He caused a fig tree to wither away by simply telling it to
He turned water into wine at a wedding celebration that had run out of wine
Healing Miracles

He healed many that were sick or handicapped:
Lepers–11
Sick and dying–8
Paralyzed–1
Blind–5
Handicapped–2
Insane–1
Deaf–1
Reattached an ear that was cut off - 1

Miracles over Demons
Cast demons into a herd of pigs
Cast demons from a mute
Cast a demon from a man in the temple
Cast out a demon from a blind and mute man, causing the man to see and speak
Raised two People from the Dead

There are so many things that He did and all of them proved that He was the Son of God but the Greatest Miracle is the most important one for us. After He died on the cross to save us from our sins He was buried. He didn't stay dead though. After three days in His tomb He rose again, proving that He could beat death and sin.

How AWESOME is that!

Closing Activity: Human Knot

Separate the kids into two teams.

Instruct each team to form a circle.

Instruct each team to do the following:

Use your right hand to grab the right hand of the person directly across from you.

Use your left hand to grab the left hand of the person to the right of the person holding your other hand.

They have now formed a human knot and, on "Go" each team will untangle, as a group, back into one open circle, without anyone letting go of hands or dislocating any joints. The first team untangled and back into a circle wins the game!

If anyone lets go they must start over.

Supplies Needed for "Impossible" Based on Funds available			
Activity	Budget	Budget w/ some frills	Bells & Whistles
Unbelievable Stand	-1 16" x 16" platform for each group of 8-10 kids	Same	Same
Unbelievable volleyball	-Some type of volleyball net -16" or larger balloon -Something inside the balloon to offer change in direction during flight -Masking tape or cones for boundaries	Same	Same
Poke or Pop	-One balloon -A Kebab stick -Vaseline	Same	Same
Straw through a potato	-Plastic straws – 1/kid -Raw potato – 1/kid -Paper towel	Same	Same
Windbag	-Diaper Genie refill or -"Windbags" – these are actually cheaper if you can find them to purchase without a shipping charge – pack of 4 is approx. $5.00. They are also colored which is more fun! -2 tables	Same	Same

Blow up a balloon with vinegar and baking soda	-½ cup vinegar -Colored soda or water bottle. -Funnel -3 tablespoons baking soda -9" colored balloon	Same	Same
Negative Inflation	-1 16 oz. soda bottle -Hot water -1 bowl -Cold water -1 pitcher or do this near a sink -1 balloon	Same	Same
Discussion	-TV/VCR or DVD player -Video or DVD depicting some of Jesus' miracles -Bible	Same	Same
Human Knot	Nothing	Nothing	Nothing

Knees

Theme Target:
Teach kids the importance of prayer and how to pray.

Golden Nugget:
When the going gets tough the tough get on their knees!

Scripture:
Matthew 6: 5–13 (New International Version and The Contemporary English Version)

For this event you could instruct kids ahead of time to bring kneepads or you could provide kneepads or gardener's kneeling boards for them because they will be on their knees a lot. Pillows would also work. Then again, so would taking their shoes off and putting them under their knees.

Activity #1: Knee-sock wars

Lay masking tape on the floor to design an "arena" and have all contestants take off shoes but leave socks on. Make it as large as you want your Nuke 'Em court for activity #3 to be. The object of this game is to keep your socks on as long as possible! There is no standing, so everyone is crawling around on the arena trying to pull everyone else's socks off while trying to defend their own socks.

Separate into two teams for the remainder of the event.

Activity #2: Stages dodgeball

Play like regular dodgeball but they are not out on the first hit–they go down to their knees and play in that position. On the second hit they sit on their buttocks. On the third hit they are out. Add a twist by stating that if they catch a ball while on their knees or on their buttocks they can go up to the next position again.

Activity #3: On Your Knees Nuke 'Em

Have the players on each team spread out on their side of the net and sit on their knees on the floor. They will now play "Nuke 'Em." If you have never heard of this it is really simple volleyball–instead of hitting it over the net they should catch the ball and throw it over the net. They can still use teamwork and toss the ball to each other before throwing over the net but, in the interest of time, only allow one toss before sending it over. This also prevents buddies from just playing together.

One point is scored for the opposite team each time the ball touches the ground. Use your own judgment on whether to charge points for the kid that is messing around and wants to play by themselves by bouncing the ball on the floor a few times or anything else like that.

Also, their knees must remain on the floor at all times. If they rise to catch the ball and they come off the floor charge a point.

Periodically, instruct them to find a new location on their side of the court. Some will try to move only a few inches, or return to a previous location. Insist that they find a location they have not been in before.

Tip: Establish pre-determined rotation locations. The first time they kneel down give each player a piece of masking tape and have them tape it to the floor. You now have the official locations for the duration of the game.

Activity #4: On Your Knees Wiffle ball

This is basic Wiffle ball but instead of running around the bases they must get on a scooter on their knees–at least one knee must be on the scooter–and move to the bases that way. All fielders, except the pitcher, should be on their knees. You decide whether they can stand to hit the ball based on their ability or provide a tee to hit off of.

Discussion: Why and how should we pray?

We've done a few activities on our knees tonight. It tends to make mobility extremely difficult. What do you think we are going to talk about with a theme like "Knees?" <Prayer>

What is prayer? <It's talking with God>

Why is it important to pray? <Communication, or talking, is the key to making any relationship good and strong. Being in a relationship with God is very special, and should be the strongest relationship you have. If you don't talk to God the relationship with Him will not be as strong as it can and should be.>

Prayer is very important. Praying to God shows Him you trust Him. It also shows Him that you need Him.

Praying should be very simple. You don't need big words. You don't need to think long and hard about what you want to tell Him. You can't tell Him anything He doesn't already know. He knows you better than anyone else ever can or will and He knows what is on your mind. Telling Him what is on your mind shows Him that you want Him to be part of it all.

You can't hide anything from God. You can't scare God. And you can't tell Him anything that will make Him stop loving you. He will never do that. The Bible tells us that nothing can separate us from His love. So, there is no need to try to keep any secrets from Him.

Jesus prayed to God many times. He knew it was important. Because it is important He taught the people around Him to pray too. This is what He said:

(Read the NIV passage first–it may be familiar to some of the kids–some may even know it already. Then read the Contemporary English Version–it is in language that is easier for kids to understand)

New International Version	Contemporary English Version
"And when you pray, do not be like the hypocrites, for they love to pray standing in the synagogues and on the street corners to be seen by men. I tell you the truth, they have received their reward in full. But when you pray, go into your room, close the door and pray to your Father, who is unseen. Then your Father, who sees what is done in secret, will reward you. And when you pray, do not keep on babbling like pagans, for they think they will be heard because of their many words. Do not be like them, for your Father knows what you need before you ask him. "This, then, is how you should pray: 'Our Father in heaven, hallowed be your name, your kingdom come, your will be done on earth as it is in heaven. Give us today our daily bread. Forgive us our debts, as we also have forgiven our debtors. And lead us not into temptation, but deliver us from the evil one.'	When you pray, don't be like those show-offs who love to stand up and pray in the meeting places and on the street corners. They do this just to look good. I can assure you that they already have their reward. When you pray, go into a room alone and close the door. Pray to your Father in private. He knows what is done in private, and he will reward you. When you pray, don't talk on and on as people do who don't know God. They think God likes to hear long prayers. Don't be like them. Your Father knows what you need before you ask. You should pray like this: Our Father in heaven, help us to honor your name. Come and set up your kingdom, so that everyone on earth will obey you, as you are obeyed in heaven. Give us our food for today. Forgive us for doing wrong, as we forgive others. Keep us from being tempted and protect us from evil.

We don't have to use those exact words when we pray. In fact, if we only used those words to pray that wouldn't tell God anything but what we memorized. But those words do tell us some things that we need to consider as we pray:

* To be respectful of Him and honor His name
* To invite Him to be with us
* To ask for help in obeying Him
* To ask for what we need and want
* To forgive us when we have done wrong
* To protect us from Satan

That's all prayer is—talking to God. Not just because we need to but also because we want to. He knows us so well that we don't even have to pray out loud. He will hear no matter what. He is never too busy for you and He is always waiting for you to talk to Him. It makes Him very happy to hear from you.

<Close with a simple prayer—you could ask the kids to pray too, if anyone wants to>

Closing Activity: Answer to Prayer Wiffle ball

This time play normal Wiffle ball. Tell them their prayers have been answered and they can play the game with full range of motion. You will have some very happy players.

For added tie-in to your discussion play an upbeat version of "The Lord's Prayer"—Carman has two great versions of this—one is a great contemporary-style and the other, while very similar, has an island flair to it.

Supplies Needed for "Knees" Based on Funds available			
Activity	Budget	Budget w/ some frills	Bells & Whistles
Knee - Sock Wars	-Masking tape to create the playing arena	Same	Same
Stages dodgeball	-Masking tape for the center line -Lots of balls that don't hurt when hit in the face or head	Same	Same
On Your Knees Nuke 'Em	-Cones -Masking tape for lines on the court and positions (if desired) -Clothesline or rope, or something to act as the net – leaders can hold it for the game -Volleyball or some type of ball to use for this	Same but with badminton or volleyball net. A pennant flag rope, like the ones seen at grand openings or on car lots, could also be used.	Same as Budget but with a freestanding volleyball or badminton net.
Knees Wiffle ball	-Bases -Wiffle Ball Bat -Wiffle Ball or soft foam ball -Batting tee (if necessary) -4 Scooter boards – these are a huge asset to your supply closet and can sometimes be purchased at Target or U.S. Toy. You can always find them for purchase on the internet They are hard plastic and approx. 18" square with handles on the side and have 4 wheels on them. These could be homemade using a wooden base, if you have a person handy with the tools.	Same but with a selection of Wiffle ball bats and soft foam balls to choose from	Same as budget w/ frills
Discussion	-Bible	Same	Same
Answer to Prayer Wiffle ball	Same as with knees Wiffle ball but without the scooters.	Same but with a selection of Wiffle ball bats and soft foam balls to choose from.	Same

Line

Theme Target:
Teach the kids about the path to Heaven.

Golden Nugget:
How do you stay on the right track?

Scripture:
John 14:6 I am the way, the truth and the life. No one comes to the Father except through me. (NIV)

Activity #1: Dragon Dodge Ball

Separate the kids into teams of four or five. Create a large circle with the kids but without the first team of four or five–they go into the center of the Dodge Ball circle. All the players on the circle must eliminate the team in the center which is the dragon. The players making up the dragon form a line, with each player putting their hands on the hips of the player in front of them. The dragon runs around trying to prevent the tail from being hit, but they cannot form a circle around the tail.

The players on the circle throw the balls at the dragon's tail, trying to hit it and eliminate it from the dragon. Any part of the dragon can be hit and not lose a player, but if the tail is hit, the tail departs from the dragon and the circle.

Once the dragon's last tail is eliminated select another team to be the new dragon. The previous dragon fills in the now empty spaces on the circle.

Activity #2: Catch Me If You Can

Put a line of masking tape down the center of the room.

Instruct the members of the largest team to get a chair and bring it to the center of the room. You will create a line of chairs, set up like musical chairs with them alternating the direction they face. There should also be one and a half chair widths in between each of them. Leave as much room as possible at the ends of the line without crowding your chairs too close. Finally, take away one chair, so there is one for each team member minus one (the remaining player is the chaser).

The other team is to line up against the wall, in whatever order they choose. They will run in that order.

It should look like this:

LINE OF WAITING RUNNERS

LOCATION TO SIT WHEN TAGGED

The team in the chairs is "it" while the other team is being chased, one at a time.

Instruct the team that got the chairs to sit down on them, keeping their feet in **front** of the chair–an important safety rule to prevent a fall from accidental (or intentional–if intentional, discipline is necessary) tripping. Select one member to be the first chaser.

Now for the tricky part... We'll start with the team being chased.

The team that is being chased will release one player at a time. That player can run anywhere in the playing court–around the ends of the chairs, through the gaps between the chairs and anywhere on either side. The rest of the team stays in their line, waiting for their turn to run. Those waiting must keep one foot against the wall at all times (this is for safety purposes as it keeps them close to the wall. Trust me the line will drift away from the wall so the kids can see what is going on. This cuts down on the running space and creates safety issues).

The kid that is being chased runs as long as possible without being tagged by the other team's runner. Once tagged the chaser immediately goes to work on catching the next runner. The next runner needs to begin running immediately so they have a better chance of getting away. A leader will need to stand at the head of the line and watch for the runner to get tagged and notify the next runner to "GO." The team being chased must pay attention so they are ready for their turn. Also, the runner being chased needs to make sure they do not get tagged close to the rest of their team. If tagged too close to the line the chaser can easily go right down the line tagging each new player before they even get a chance to run.

Instruct the players that once tagged they are out and must sit or stand against the wall on the other side of the room.

The team that is "It" must only have one person running at a time, that runner is the chaser. Unfortunately, the chaser can only chase on one side of the chair line. If the runner crosses the line, either by running around it on either end or by running through it in a gap between chairs, the chaser must tap the shoulder of one of his teammates that is sitting in a chair facing the side that the runner is now on. The chaser cannot cross over the line. Once a new chaser is tapped and leaves their chair the retired chaser sits in the now empty seat and waits to be tapped again.

Keep a stopwatch running during each round. The team that lasts longer without all being tagged wins the round. The kids will want to play several rounds.

If this is the first time you are playing this game there are two important things to do:

Run the first round slowly so the kids get the hang of it. It may take the entire first round for them to remember to only run on their side, to use the gaps in the chairs, to not run full steam if it is not necessary (I have seen savvy kids eat up lots of time by not running much at all but, rather, just staying close to the chair line and crossing over far enough to be out of reach—utilizing the rule for chasers to not cross over).

1. Realize that this will not be the last time you play this game

2. Be aware that you may use a lot of time explaining this game. It is difficult to explain without using examples, but once the kids know how to play it is a blast and will surely become a favorite.

Activity #3: Line Soccer

Within the teams, starting with the smallest kid, assign each player on each team a number, one through the highest number of players on the largest team. If teams are uneven choose kids to be multiple numbers and then be careful not to call those numbers together–unless the other team is losing really bad and needs an advantage. Yes, you have the right to do that!

Place a ball in the center of the two teams. When you call a number the players with that number run out and try to kick the ball across the other team's line. The line is involved in preventing the ball from crossing the line by blocking it with their bodies. The line can catch the ball or knock it down. The line can only block the ball it cannot throw or kick the ball and score by putting it through the other team's line.

Activity #4: Catch the Dragon's Tail

All the players line up and put their hands on the waist of the person in front of them. The last person in line tucks one end of a bandana or scarf in his back pocket, belt, or waistband. The first person in line tries to grab the scarf. When the "head" gets the "tail," he dons the scarf and becomes the new tail. The person second in line becomes the head.

Variation: Break into teams of at least two kids each and have them create their own dragon, giving each team a scarf or bandana. The tail puts it in their back pocket or tucks it into the back of their pants, leaving plenty hanging freely.

Each team now runs around attempting to catch another team's tail, but only the head of the dragon can remove the tail. The dragon must remain together at all times. A tail removed by a dragon that is missing pieces does not count.

Once a team's tail is gone the team is out. The team that collects the most tails, not the team that is left standing at the end, is the winner of the round.

Discussion: How do you tow the line?

You will need a roll of white paper, a thick-tipped black marker and a "Line Chaserz" car. If you cannot find the car or do not have the budget for it see the alternative noted at the end of the discussion.

Open the discussion with the opening scene of "A Bug's Life"–when the ants are all carrying their offerings to the offering stone in a single file line. A leaf falls and breaks up the line. The ants panic because the line has broken and they no longer know where to go. Watch until they get the line going again and are greatly relieved that they have found their direction again.

Ask the question: *"Why did the ants panic?"*
We all need to follow somebody's lead right? When we are little we rely on someone to teach us how to do basic things. We aren't born knowing how to dress ourselves, tie our shoes, or anything else that you now do on your own.

We don't teach ourselves how to read or write. We don't teach ourselves how to cook or work or anything else that we need to do to survive. We rely on someone to show us or lead us in the right direction.

<Take out a roll of paper–you want it to unroll to be at least five feet long>

Unroll the paper and have the kids sit on the floor along the edge. Instruct them not to step on or crinkle the paper.

**Reveal your "Line Chaserz" car.

Imagine you are driving a car, but nobody has ever taught you how to drive or how to get where you are going. It might look like this... <Put the car on the blank paper and turn it on—the car will drive sporadically with no line to follow.>

<Pick up the car> *It takes someone to teach you how to drive before you can even go in a straight line.*

Have a kid draw a relatively straight line with the black marker (not too long–don't use all your paper).

When someone teaches us how to do something we are able to do it much sooner, and with better results than when we attempt to do something on our own. <Place the car on the paper at the line and turn it on. The car will now follow the line steadily until it reaches the end. Pick up the car>

That is exactly how it is in the path to Heaven. Jesus says in the Bible, "I am the way, the truth and the life. No one comes to the Father except through me." Does anyone know what that means? (Accepting Jesus is the only way to enter into the kingdom of God).

So, we must follow Him in order to get to Heaven. So, how do we follow Him?

(First we must accept Him as our Lord and Savior and then we must watch and listen for His leading)

We can't follow Him if nobody tells us about Him. There is no way to "just know" who Jesus is. Somebody needs to introduce us to Him. Once we are introduced, there is no way to follow Him without knowing how to do so. We learn through instruction. What are some ways that we can learn about Jesus? (Bible, teachers, church, etc.)

So, following Jesus requires listening to instruction. When Jesus says to "Follow Me" we need to listen to His leading. How does He lead us? (He speaks to us through His word and the Holy Spirit)

Does Jesus promise to take us on a nice straight path like this one that we drew? (No)

Have a kid, or several, add to the line, making it curve all around the paper–be sure they keep it thick enough for the car to "read" it. If the line crosses at some point the car will have trouble following the direction and will get "stuck" that's ok–work that into your discussion and explain that sometimes God gives us a choice of which direction to take. The trick is to stay focused on Him and make a decision based on what you feel Him leading you to do.

Place the car on the paper near the beginning of the straight part of the line and turn it on. The car will travel the path as it is drawn.

At some point, perhaps when the car reaches an intersection and doesn't know what to do (but after you have explained about choices), take the car off course, or let it run out of line. Explain that what happens to the car is what it also feels like when we take our focus off of God's leading and try to lead ourselves. Our path is never as good as the one God has designed for us and if we try to make our own way we end up in circles or, worse, we stall out completely.

Challenge the kids to follow the path God has for them by focusing on Jesus. It might not always be easy but it is definitely the best choice and way better than wandering around aimlessly.

**If you do not have, can't afford, or can't find the Line Chaserz Car, you can accomplish the same thing with magnets–but your set-up will require another person. Use a glass-top table or set up a "table" using a box with a see-through top of some sort. Use a table skirt around the edges–you will need someone to hide inside this area. Cover the top of the see-through area with your paper–so none of the kids see the person inside.

The intent here is for the person inside to be able to see the line as it is drawn and be able to follow it with a magnet. Make sure the magnet is strong enough to draw your object to it through the table and the paper. A car that responds to the magnet is the best object to use because of the wheels moving much easier. Practice this ahead of time so you get the best effect!

This is a great opportunity to offer an invitation to accept Jesus. You need to be ready to offer one at anytime it is appropriate, and you need to be extremely comfortable with the words you use to share it. If you have not done so already prepare, in your own words, the words for your invitation. Remember, it needs to be simple for kids to understand, sincere in

its tone and succinct in its delivery. For an example of an invitation you will find one in the "Salvation Invitation" section of this book.

If anyone accepts your invitation and asks Jesus into their heart for the first time please make it a special celebration with the rest of the group. It's not a time for embarrassment but they should be aware of their awesome step of faith. Tell them that there is a party in Heaven at that moment for the place that has been reserved for them!

Closing Activity: Sumo Tube

Make a square–approximately 12' x 12' to use as the playing area. Each team should be standing or sitting well outside of the playing square.

When you call a number the kid on each team that has that number comes to the center. You will give each one of them an inner tube and have them hold it around their waist. Once "tubed" up insist that they honor their opponent by bowing (You will have some kids that really play this up and bow like a sumo wrestler would–which is great fun).

Ask each one, individually, "Are you ready to rumble?" When you have received a "yes" from each one yell, "Go!"

On "go" they will each try to push the other one out of the playing area with their inner tube. They must keep both hands on the tube at all times so as not to push or hit with their hands. If a fall occurs pause the play and let the fallen player get up and reset.

The first player to step over the line of the playing box, if even just a toe, is the loser and both return to their team.

The kids will LOVE this game, and after all have gone, they will most likely ask if they can challenge a specific player. Allow this as you have time and as long as the other player accepts the challenge.

Supplies Needed for "Line" Based on Funds available

Activity	Budget	Budget w/ some frills	Bells & Whistles
Dragon Dodge Ball	-Soft balls that don't hurt if hit in the face or head	Same	Same
Catch Me If You Can	-Masking tape for center line -Chairs -Stopwatch -Whistle	Same	Same
Line Soccer	-Cones for boundaries -Masking tape for lines -Kickball	Same	Same
Catch the Dragon's Tail	-1 bandana per team	Same	Same
Discussion	-TV & VCR or DVD Player -Bug's Life video or DVD -Table w/ see-through top -Table skirt -Strong magnet -Car that reacts to magnet	Same but "Line Chasers" toy car instead of table, skirt, magnet and car that reacts to magnet "Line Chasers" cars are sold in Toys 'R Us or other toy stores or can be purchased on the Internet.	
Sumo Tube	-Masking tape -2 inner tubes – real or plastic inflatable pool rings	Same	Same

Nasty

Theme Target:
Teach kids that Satan is always lurking, waiting to get in our way.

Golden Nugget:
Dealing with that slimy devil is a Nasty job!

Scripture:
Matthew 4:10–11 (NIV)

Kids should be forewarned to wear old clothes and sneakers, and bring a towel and change of clothes for their ride home.

Separate kids into two teams for the event.

Activity #1: Eat Your Vegetables

You can play this two different ways. One is a team play and the other is not.

Team play:

Provide several plates of baby food vegetables and spoons. I know you just realized where this is going and can't believe what is being suggested here; however, trust me, this will be a perfect opener to this theme. You may even have a few kids say, "This is so nasty!"–a perfect segue into your theme.

You determine the level of nastiness on this one with the type of vegetable you choose. Some of them look nasty but aren't bad at all–like sweet potatoes or a combination of sweet potatoes and corn. The fruits or desserts can be pretty yummy, so it is just mind over matter on that one. For a ton of fun try broccoli and cauliflower–it actually tastes good but looks hideous. Obviously you need to be concerned about allergies. Hopefully you know all food allergies up front and can plan accordingly from the start. Otherwise, have kids with allergies sit out on this one.

You will basically have the teams compete to see which team can clean their plates the fastest. You will have some kids that actually like the stuff–their team will depend on them heavily. You may also have some kids that you are concerned about hurling–don't be alarmed, just try to do this activity outside.

Individual play:

Have all kids stand or sit in a circle. Provide several jars of baby food, with the labels off, and a spoon in each one to start. Play just like musical chairs but with passing the jar around instead. When the music stops, the kid left holding the jar, or with more of a hand on it, has to eat a spoonful. Replace the spoon with a new one and play the next round. Play as long as you'd like or until the first sign of vomiting.

Activity #2: Nasty Sculpture

This requires a good sport on each team.

For each team provide: a shower cap or bathing cap; some peanut butter (make sure no peanut allergies) or whipped cream or something else that is easily spread; plastic knives or spoons; and a container of "goldfish" snacks or cheerios or something else that is small and lightweight.

On "Go" each team will spread the goo all over the shower cap. For more control the leaders can do this instead. Once spread, the team members will have a specific amount of time–five minutes or whatever you choose–to apply the stickable items to the goo, attempting to make a better creation than the opposing team. At the end of the time judge the creations on whatever criteria you chose, such as: creativity; height; amount of stickable items; stability; etc.

Have towels and washcloths handy for clean up.

Activity #3: Jelly Blow

You will need some clear plastic tubing for this game–in lengths of approximately eight inches per two kids. You could also use your marshmallow shooters from other events in this book.

Bend the tube and squirt some jelly into the center of it.

Within the teams, starting with the smallest kid, assign each player on each team a number, one through the highest number of players on the largest team. If teams are uneven some kids on the smaller teams will need more than one number. When you call a number the player on each team with that number comes to the center. They will each put their mouth on one end of the tube–don't allow them to take big breath first. On "Go" they will each begin blowing as hard as they can, trying to project the jelly through the tube and onto their opponent.

This is great fun since you will most likely have at least one kid that decides to take their mouth off and take a big breath. A smart opponent will seize that opportunity and send that jelly through the tube so fast that kid won't know what hit them. Well, obviously they will know it is jelly.

Activity #4: Twisted Twister

Make up your own twister mat using a disposable plastic dropcloth. Using some nasty condiments make the colored dots–one set of dots for each player. You may need several drop cloths–unless you choose to make this an up-front game vs. an all play.

The dots can be made of tempera paint, or for an added "twist" you could opt for the following:

* Yellow–Mustard

* Red–Ketchup

* Blue–Grape Jelly

* Green–Mint Jelly, Jello or pistachio pudding

Make the dots as thick as you desire.

Instruct players to remove shoes and socks and roll up pant legs and shirtsleeves. Now, play twister according to the normal rules. If you don't have access to an actual twister game you will need to make a spinner or devise some way of selecting the action to be taken.

Activity #5: William Tell

One kid from each team is to serve as the target. The team will make a circle and the target will sit in a chair in the middle of the circle. On his head put a good sized dollop of "No-tears shampoo foam." This comes in a pump bottle that will give you a nice stiff ball of shampoo. You could also use shaving cream but would need to provide goggles for the kid to protect their eyes.

Each player is given a squirt gun that will shoot a good stream of water. Provide each team with a bucket of water to refill as necessary. You could also use bottles of water with a squirter on it–or clean spray bottles that have the ability to squirt a stream of water vs. a spray.

On "Go" all kids begin squirting their guns at the player in the center, trying to rinse the shampoo away.

If you don't have enough squirt guns this could be done with two good squirt guns or super soakers, with a large reservoir for the water. The squirt gun will be given to one kid who will take three shots. He then passes it to the next player in the circle, and so on and so on. The first team to satisfactorily rinse the shampoo off the kid's head wins the game.

Activity #6: Spew

This game is an "Every-Man-For-Himself" game. You definitely want to do this outside or in a place that you can just hose down afterward.

This game is so much fun to watch–you may want to videotape it for your future enjoyment.

Provide each kid with an antacid tablet like alka seltzer and a small cup or can of clear soda. If the antacid tablets are individually wrapped, unwrap enough for each kid and put them in a candy dish to disguise what they really are.

On "Go" each kid is to pop the tablet into their mouth and put it under their tongue. They are then to take a big swig of soda and keep it in their mouth. They must close their mouth immediately after doing so. The object of the game is to keep the contents of their mouth from spilling out.

You will have some macho boys that think this is really easy. Much to their surprise it is way more difficult than they can imagine.

The last five kids (or whatever number you choose) with the contents still in their mouth should be given a prize.

Discussion: Satan is a slimy devil.

The discussion will take place while creating slime—see recipe below. This stuff is seriously cool—think of the slime you bought at the store in a small container and played with as a kid, or last week if you are like me. When mixed up correctly and combined it feels really cool but doesn't stick to skin—think of not quite firm jello. This slime is completely safe. Guar gum is actually edible. It is like cornstarch on steroids.

You should have the components of it made up ahead of time and make a huge batch in a large container or baby pool for your discussion, or bring all the ingredients, which are few, and allow each kid to make their own slime to take home. You could also do both.

There are two mixtures that combine to make the slime. You will need to make the two parts to the slime mixture ahead of time. Put them in separate buckets/containers with lids. It is recommended that the Borax solution be made the same day as your event–otherwise all the borax may settle to the bottom of the container and be very difficult to stir back into the water.

First make a saturated Borax solution by mixing about one cup of Borax (Found in laundry section of grocery store) with about six and a half cups of warm water. Stir the solution. (If all of the powder dissolves, add more until no more will dissolve). *This is enough solution for over six batches of the guar gum mixture. Only make one batch of this to six batches of the other–then take out ½ cup of this solution for each batch since it is extra. If you forget that this is way more than you need for one batch your slime will be too runny.

Measure four cups of warm water into a large mixing bowl. If you want colored slime add food coloring to the water now. SLOWLY (very slowly) stir in two teaspoons of guar gum. This fine powder has a tendency to clump up if it is not stirred into the water slowly. After thoroughly mixing, pour the guar gum mixture into a bucket with a lid for transport. Unfortunately, if you try to make this in bigger batches it is too difficult to mix it properly. I have found it much easier to mix it in batches of two cups water and one teaspoon guar gum powder in a shaker. Once mixed you can dump it all into the same container and stir it all together. Try both ways and see which one works better.

When combining these two to get the slime you will add one cup of the Borax water solution to each four-cup batch of the guar gum mixture. Wait for a few seconds and then stir it up.

Keep track of your amounts so you can dump the entire contents of the Borax solution bucket into the guar gum mixture you have created.

Be sure to try this ahead of time so you know how it combines together. *You will be amazed!* And just think how your kids will react. Note: This stuff gets really thick and should not be poured down a drain. For clean up—either dump or scoop into trash bag and throw out–double bag it, or dump on the ground and hose it down. All ingredients are safe for environment and will not harm anything–but will sure look gross to someone that did not participate in your experiment.

Now for the fun part!

Set up a kiddie pool or large container–something big enough for a few kids to get their hands into. Obviously, the bigger it is the more kids can mix it up but you will also need more of the mixtures.

Now for the actual discussion:

Open with a question:
What is the "Nastiest" thing you can think of? (You should get some pretty interesting answers here)

Share with the kids something you think is really nasty. Try to really disgust them.

Satan is pretty nasty isn't he? He works hard to seep into our lives and mess us up. He lies to us and makes us think things we shouldn't. He wants to make us believe that God doesn't love us—which is the biggest lie ever. He tries to make us think things are really cool that aren't. He tries to make us believe that things that can really hurt us are exactly what we need.

He is one slimy devil!

Select a few kids to put their hands in the pool or container.

We go along, minding our own business and that's when Satan creeps in. <Pour the bucket of guar gum mixture into the pool over the unsuspecting hands. You will get a great reaction and all the kids watching will want to put their hands in. Allow them to if you have room but instruct them not to slosh it around too much, or worse, throw it at each other—which will be a great temptation. Again, it won't hurt anyone but it may make someone angry or start a war that you don't want>.

That Satan is so slimy he gets all over everything. Then, everything you touch gets all nasty and you can't get him off.

So, what should you do? (See what kind of suggestions you get here— pray is the one you are looking for)

God has given us exactly what we need to get that slimy devil junk off of us. He gave us His Son, Jesus, to defeat the devil. When we look to Jesus to guide us He defeats that slimy devil with His power. <Pour the Borax solution over the hands and into the pool>

You gotta' keep Jesus in every area of your life. <Get them to swish it around—within a few seconds the solutions will react and the slime should start peeling off their hands>

Jesus Himself was tempted by Satan. Jesus spent some time in the desert and Satan came along to try to get Jesus to sin. He made several suggestions to Jesus in his attempts to get Jesus to prove something to Him. If Jesus had done it He would have been playing into Satan's plan and would have sinned against God.

After a few unsuccessful tries to get Jesus to sin Satan finally took Jesus to the top of a high mountain where he could see the whole world. He said to Jesus, "I will give you everything you see if you bow down and worship me."

Jesus said to him, "Away from me, Satan! For it is written: 'Worship the Lord your God, and serve him only.'" Then the devil left him, and angels came and attended him.

We need to follow Jesus' example when Satan creeps in and tries to get us to do things we know we shouldn't. You just gotta' say—"Get Thee Behind Me Slimy Devil! I got Jesus in my life!"

If you desire and you have time—allow each kid to make their own small batch of slime in a plastic bag or give them each a cupful from the kiddie pool or container.

To make in a small batch for each kid:

* ✶ Make enough Borax solution for all the kids ahead of time.

* ✶ In their Ziploc bag each kid should put one cup of water, food coloring (as desired) and ½ teaspoon guar gum powder. Seal the bag and have them shake it or knead it until the powder is mixed in and it thickens.

* ✶ Open the bag and add two, to two-and-a half tsp. of the Borax solution.

* ✶ Re-seal the bag and mix together to form the slime.

Closing Activity: Nasty water balloon toss

Who doesn't love a good old water balloon game?

For this activity you will fill a bunch of water balloons—at least one per kid—with a mixture of water and something else, depending on how

"Nasty" you wanna' be. A few really nasty suggestions: tomato juice; sauerkraut juice; or clamato juice, you get the idea. A few other nasty suggestions, though not as thoroughly gross: Water with a sardine in each balloon; water with a worm in it; water with some solid object in it that will freak them out when it is on them.

Since this is the last activity of the event and you have discussed how slimy Satan is you could also work off of that. You could fill the balloons with the slime—pretty nasty! You could also fill the balloons with a solution of water and baby shampoo—which will not hurt their eyes and will also symbolize washing Satan's filth off of you.

Once you decide the direction you want to take with this and have all of your balloons in a bucket or container you are ready to play.

As in "Jelly Blow" each player on each team has a number. Each team should line up on their side of the playing area.

You can play this several ways:

★ In the center of your playing area place two water balloons to start the round. Call out a number. As soon as they hear the number the kid on each team that has that number runs to the center and picks up a balloon as fast as they can. They then attempt to hit the other player with it before they get hit themselves. The first one to get the other one wet wins the round. If dodged it doesn't count as a score.

★ Have each line spread out (a few feet between each team member) and then move in close, with the numbers on each side paired up. Picture a line of square dancers, partners across from each other, that are close enough to form an arch tunnel by raising their hands together in the center, but each pair is far enough away that they cannot touch the teammate on either side of them. If teams are uneven you will need a willing leader to participate in this.

Give each pair a water balloon, staggering the team in each pair that begins with the balloon. Now it is just like the old-fashioned water balloon toss. Players begin tossing and, with every catch, take another step backward. The team with the least number of "ballooned" players wins the game.

Supplies Needed for "Nasty" Based on Funds available			
Activity	Budget	Budget w/ some frills	Bells & Whistles
Eat Your Vegetables	-2 jars of baby food -If musical food - 1 spoon per jar – per round you want to play -CD player and CD -If team play – 1 spoon per player and a paper plate for each type of baby food	Same but with several jars of baby food	Same but add 1 bib for each player
Nasty Sculpture	-Supply of Peanut Butter or whipped cream for each team -Supply of "goldfish", cheerios or other small stickable item for each team -2 bathing or shower caps (Saran Wrap covers, size medium, also work) -Washcloths -Towels	Same	Same
Jelly Blow	-Plastic tubing or marshmallow shooters from previous themes -Duct tape or clear strong tape (if using the shooters – you tape them together) -Jelly in a squeeze bottle -Cooler	Same	Same
Twisted Twister	-Disposable plastic dropcloth – 1 per twister mat -Tempera paint for Dot making -Spinner -Washcloths or Baby wipes - CD player and CD with "The Twist" or "Twist and Shout" playing	Same	Same but with either tempera paint or nastier ingredients: Mustard; ketchup; grape jelly and mint jelly, green jello or pistachio pudding. Also, CD player and CD with "The Twist" or "Twist and Shout" playing

William Tell	-Shaving cream -2 pairs goggles -2 good squirt guns; 2 clean squirt bottles with ability to squirt a stream vs. a spray; or 2 water bottles with squirter -2 Buckets of water -2 chairs -2 towels	-Shaving cream or No-tears pump shampoo -2 super soakers with good-sized water reservoir -2 chairs -2 towels	-No-tears pump shampoo -1 good squirt gun for each player -2 chairs -2 towels -2 buckets of water to refill their guns, if necessary
Spew	-1 effervescent antacid tablet (alka seltzer) per player -1 Dixie cup of clear soda per player	Same	Same
Discussion	-Kiddie pool or large container -Buckets of pre-mixed slime ingredients	Same plus additional ingredients for each kid to make their own slime and small Ziploc bag to make it in.	Same as budget w/ frills but use kiddie pool so all kids can help mix slime with hands or feet.
Nasty water balloon toss	-Water balloons filled with mixture of your choice. -Buckets	Same	Same

Obstacles/Influence

Theme Target:
Teach kids about obstacles that are in their paths and how to overcome them.

Golden Nugget:
Whose influence do you follow to get past obstacles in life?

Scripture:
Story of Job (The Message)

In this event you will set up an obstacle course with many activities within it–at least six different things to do. It is best to have two teams competing against each other, requiring you to have two of every activity set up. If you do not have the supplies to do so you could run another activity simultaneously, having one team perform in the course and the other participating in the other activity and then switching.

A great way to make your point about facing obstacles with no positive influence would be to blindfold the participant in the obstacle course and have them work their way through it, relying on a teammate to guide them through. You could throw in another element and allow one player from the opposing team to offer negative influence–giving bad directions, making lots of noise to disrupt concentration. Another obstacle would be to have music playing loudly that has a driving beat to it.

After your discussion the teams can really compete in the course with no blindfolds. Drives the point home of the positive results you achieve when you are able to keep focused as you are faced with obstacles.

Obstacle course:

You will need a defined starting and finishing line. In the blindfolded competition you can release players as the previous player completes the first two obstacles–if you have enough blindfolds to do so. This may create a bottleneck at one or more obstacles–making your point stronger.

Designate which side each team must stay to in each obstacle by color-coding the obstacles and the teams with a distinguishing mark, so there is no confusion when they approach the obstacle. This can be done simply with a colored arrow cut from paper and taped down at each obstacle.

In the blindfolded run the player does not retrieve balls and make it ready for the next player. You will either need the "influencer" to do that or a leader stationed there for that purpose.

Obstacle #1: Military crawl

Set up two rows of, at lest four, chairs in parallel lines, with enough distance between them to allow for two players to crawl through side by side. Using clothesline rope or yarn, string it across the open space attaching it to and winding around the chairs at seat level. No cutting of the rope will be necessary in this case.

Obstacle #2: Climb over an obstacle

A few feet from the end of the rope crawl place an old couch, folding chairs or other obstacle to climb over, with the back facing the player when they emerge from the ropes.

Obstacle #3: Throw balls at a stack of cups to knock them over - Bonus points offered at this obstacle.

Stack three cups on a table for each team. Provide two or three balls per team and place them on the floor at the throwing line (a strip of masking tape)–several feet from the table. They can throw as many balls as provided in attempt to knock over the cups–additional points are awarded for each cup actually knocked over. If you do not have a leader assigned to collect the balls the player must collect what they have thrown and put them back at the mark for the next player, before moving on to the next obstacle.

Award bonus points for a successful attempt.

Obstacle #4: Throw football or soft foam ball through a hoop - Bonus points offered at this obstacle.

Suspend a hula-hoop in the air for each team. If you have no means of doing so a leader could hold them, or attach them to the wall or lean them against a stationary object. Lay down a strip of masking tape at the distance from the hoop that you would like them to throw and place the ball on the line. The player approaches the throwing line, picks up the ball and attempts to throw it through the hoop. The player must then retrieve the ball and place it back on the line.

Award bonus points for a successful attempt.

Obstacle #4: Kick a ball through a goal that has an obstacle in the center of it -Bonus points offered at this obstacle.

For this one you could get away with having only one goal. Set up a goal using two cones and place an obstacle in the center–a chair, a leader, a bop bag. If this obstacle is in a corner it will save some room. Both players can kick at the same time–place a mark on the floor where the ball must be spotted for the kick–so that they each have the same angle they are kicking from and don't move the ball to benefit themselves and hinder their opponent.

Award bonus points for a successful attempt.

Obstacle #5: Hockey Shot -Bonus points could be offered at this obstacle.

Provide one kid's hockey stick and one soft foam ball at the shooting line for each team. At the line they take a shot on goal—a laundry basket on its side. You decide whether they must continue shooting until they make it or they get one shot and bonus points if it goes in. On the blind-folded attempt it should be just one attempt.

They retrieve the ball and place it, and the stick, back on the line for the next player.

Award bonus points for a successful attempt.

Obstacle #6: Balance Beam

Set up a small balance beam for each team. A 2 x 4 laid on a few bricks is simple and won't be too high for an injury to occur–especially for the blindfolded run.

This should be self-explanatory.

Obstacle #7: Putt-putt -Bonus points offered at this obstacle.

Place a golf ball on a designated spot for each team and lay a putter next to it–real or toy, either is fine. Tape down a plastic cup for each team, with the lip cut off of one side of each one–to allow it to lay flat. You determine how many putts they get to put it in. If only one attempt offer bonus points for a hole in one. They must retrieve the ball and place it on the mark, along with the putter. For ease of retrieval you could lay down a few brooms allowing the sticks to serve as barriers.

Award bonus points for a hole-in-one.

Obstacle #8: Shoot a Basket -Bonus points could be offered at this obstacle.

Provide one ball per team at the shooting line (strip of masking tape on the floor). Upon approaching the line they pick up the ball and attempt to make a basket. If you don't have an actual basket, no worries—use a hamper; trash can or position this obstacle at a door and put up one of those door hanger hoops for each team. You decide whether they get one shot and bonus points for making it or whether they keep shooting until they make it.

Obstacle #9: Scooter slalom

Set up an identical, simple slalom, using a few cones, for each team. Provide a scooter (razor or platform) or a skateboard for each team. From the starting point they must successfully maneuver the scooter through the slalom. A leader will need to take the scooter back to the starting point for the next player.

Obstacle #10: Pop a balloon by sitting on it

If you do not want to blow up enough balloons to provide two per player you can accomplish this task at the beginning of the event. Give each kid two balloons to blow up and tie off. Each team then places their balloons in a trash bag.

At the start of the blindfolded run of the obstacle course empty one bag of balloons onto the ground/floor in your area for this obstacle.

Upon the approach to this obstacle the player must grab a balloon and place it on the ground/floor. They then proceed to pop it by sitting on it. You may need to have a pin handy for the player that is stuck with one of those balloons that are not fully inflated and extremely difficult to pop. **Note: This is so much fun to watch in the blindfolded run.

Once the balloon pops the player proceeds to the finish line.

★ Alternate Activity to run simultaneously with course or Closing Activity:

Obstacle Fly Swatter Hockey or Soccer

Set up a hockey arena with cones to create the goals. Place some obstacles in the playing area–bop bags, chairs, anything really.

Separate into two equal teams and provide one fly swatter per player. Using a ping-pong ball, or other small safe ball, proceed to play hockey according to all normal hockey rules. Note: If you use a ping-pong ball you will need extras on hand since they only last until stepped on.

If you don't have enough fly swatters play regular soccer.

Discussion: What influences you when faced with obstacles?

Show a clip from "Cast Away"–the scene right after the plane has crashed and he is deserted on the island. Watch long enough to see that he is having great difficulty getting food, water, shelter, etc. and must learn to survive. He opens the packages that he collected and then finds ways to use them to provide for himself.

We didn't see the beginning of the movie but that was a guy that had a great life. He was successful. He was engaged to a great woman. They had a great place to live. He was very happy and most people would have been very happy with his life.

Then, his plane crashed and he was left alone, with practically nothing to survive. He had lost everything, but his life. He was in big trouble.

No matter where he looked there was no way out. If he was going to survive he was going to have to learn how to use what was available to him. Nothing was going to be easy. He just needed to focus on living. Happiness was out of reach.

What would you have done?

There is a story in the Bible about a guy that had everything. His name was Job.

He was rich. He had a big family–a loving wife and ten kids. He had lots of land and animals. In Bible times having a lot of animals was a great thing–the more you had the better off you were considered to be. This guy had hundreds of many kinds of animals. He had lots of servants and was considered to be the most influential man in the land.

Job was a great man too. He was very honest and was totally devoted to God. He hated evil with a passion. He was so good that he would even pray for the forgiveness of his children's sins when they would throw wild parties. The day after a party he would go and pray and offer a sacrifice for his children, in case they had committed sins during their party.

Job had everything and he deserved it. His life couldn't get any better. But it was about to get a lot worse.

This is how the story is told in the book of Job chapter 1:6–19 (The Message):

> One day when the angels came to report to God, Satan, who was the Designated Accuser, came along with them. God singled out Satan and said, "What have you been up to?"
>
> Satan answered God, "Going here and there, checking things out on earth."
>
> God said to Satan, "Have you noticed my friend Job? There's no one quite like him—honest and true to his word, totally devoted to God and hating evil."
>
> Satan retorted, "So do you think Job does all that out of the sheer goodness of his heart? Why, no one ever had it so good! You pamper him like a pet, make sure nothing bad ever happens to him or his family or his possessions, bless everything he does—he can't lose!
>
> "But what do you think would happen if you reached down and took away everything that is his? He'd curse you right to your face, that's what."
>
> God replied, "We'll see. Go ahead—do what you want with all that is his. Just don't hurt him." Then Satan left the presence of God.
>
> Sometime later, while Job's children were having one of their parties at the home of the oldest son, a messenger came to Job and said, "The oxen were plowing and the donkeys grazing in the field next to us when Sabeans attacked. They stole the animals and killed the field hands. I'm the only one to get out alive and tell you what happened."
>
> While he was still talking, another messenger arrived and said,

"Bolts of lightning struck the sheep and the shepherds and fried them—burned them to a crisp. I'm the only one to get out alive and tell you what happened."

While he was still talking, another messenger arrived and said, "Chaldeans coming from three directions raided the camels and massacred the camel drivers. I'm the only one to get out alive and tell you what happened."

While he was still talking, another messenger arrived and said, "Your children were having a party at the home of the oldest brother when a tornado swept in off the desert and struck the house. It collapsed on the young people and they died. I'm the only one to get out alive and tell you what happened."

Job got to his feet, ripped his robe, shaved his head, then fell to the ground and worshiped: Naked I came from my mother's womb, naked I'll return to the womb of the earth. God gives, God takes. God's name be ever blessed.

Not once through all this did Job sin; not once did he blame God.

The story continues with Satan telling God that Job would curse God if he no longer had his health. So God allowed Satan to do what he wanted but he was not allowed to kill Job.

So, Satan left God and struck Job with terrible sores. Job was covered with ulcers and scabs from head to foot. They itched and oozed so badly that he took a piece of broken pottery to scrape himself, then went and sat on a trash heap, among the ashes.

His wife said, "Still holding on to your precious integrity, are you? Curse God and be done with it!"

He told her, "You're talking like an empty-headed fool. We take the good days from God—why not also the bad days?"

Not once through all this did Job sin. He said nothing against God. He did become discouraged and wondered why he was born. He did not understand why all of this was happening to him. He didn't think it was fair, but he did not curse God. Even when his wife suggested he just tell God he hated Him so God would kill him and get it over with.

But Job refused. He realized that God had given him everything good in His life and if God decided to take it away that He must have a good reason. He would be patient and do his best to get through the bad things he was given in life too.

Job did not allow himself to be influenced by evil or by those who told him to just turn his back on God. Despite all the obstacles that Satan put in his path Job continued to walk with God.

If you were Job what would you have done?

Have you had any obstacles in your life that you have had to get over or around?

What influences you at those times?

In the future will you listen to those that tell you to take the easy way out or will you pray to God and be patient as you go through the hard times?

It can be hard to stay focused on God when you want to give up.

Wanna' know what happened to Job in the end? God rewarded Him for being faithful despite Satan's attempts to make him curse God.

At the end of the story God blessed Job's later life even more than his earlier life. He ended up with fourteen thousand sheep, six thousand camels, one thousand teams of oxen, and one thousand donkeys. He also had seven more sons and three more daughters.

WOW! What a story.

God never promised Job he would be so greatly rewarded for being faithful. He doesn't promise us that type of reward either, but being faithful to God will definitely offer great reward to you in the form that God sees best for you.

Be faithful when you are faced with obstacles and allow God's influence to control you.

Closing Activity

Either play **Obstacle Fly Swatter Hockey** (detailed above) if not played simultaneously with the Obstacle Course, or run through the **Obstacle Course** again, without blindfolds, to see how the time has changed.

Supplies for "Obstacles and Influence" Based on Funds available			
Activity	Budget	Budget w/ some frills	Bells & Whistles
General	-Masking Tape for lines -Stopwatch -Blindfolds	Same	Same
Crawl under ropes	-8 – 10 Chairs -Rope	Same	Same
Climb over a couch	-2 Folding Chairs or a couch	Same	Same
Knock over a stack of cups	-Table -6 plastic cups -6 safe balls to throw	Same	Same
Throw football through hoop	-2 footballs -2 hula-hoops -Stands to suspend them -Duct tape	Same	Same
Kick a ball through goal with obstacle in front of it	-2 balls -2 cones -Folding chair	-2 balls -2 cones -Bop Bag	-2 Balls -2 goals -2 Bop Bags
Hockey shot	-2 hockey sticks -2 safe balls -2 laundry baskets or goals	Same	Same
Balance Beam	-2 balance beam planks -Bricks to elevate the planks	Same	Same
Putt-Putt	-2 cups -2 putters -2 golf balls -Brooms for barriers -Duct tape	Same	Same

Shoot into basket	-2 balls -2 baskets (hampers; trashcans; door hanger hoops)	Same	Same
Scooter slalom	-2 scooters (Razor style or platform) or skateboards -Cones	Same	Same
Pop a balloon	-2 balloons per player -2 trash bags	Same	Same
Discussion	-TV/VCR or DVD player -Vide or DVD of "CastAway" -Bible	Same	Same

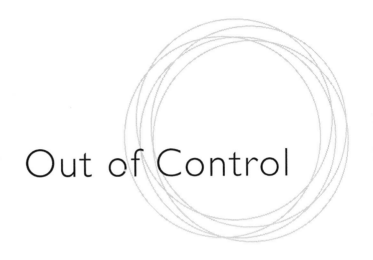

Out of Control

Theme Target:
Teach kids about the power of Jesus/God over all.

Golden Nugget:
God controls the storms in our lives.

Scripture:
Calming the storm–Matthew 8:23–27 (NIV)

Separate into two teams for the event.

Activity #1: Crack the Whip

This is a relay race. You will want to do this one in future events–it is a blast to watch!

Within the teams the players need to have a partner. Provide each team with a scooter and a jump rope. Each pair will take their turn in the relay–one player will sit, kneel, or lay on the scooter–No Standing allowed! That player will also grab on to the rope. The other player will pull the one on the scooter to the other side of the room, around the cone that is set up, and back to their team's line. Once they both cross the line the next pair gets the scooter and the rope. Do this twice through, switching which partner does which on the second round. The first team finished, that is sitting quietly, wins the game.

Teams may figure out they can tie the rope to the scooter instead of holding on to it while they ride. Allow them to do this if you want to.

Don't allow the next pair to begin until the runner and the scooter rider have crossed the line!

Smaller kids have an obvious advantage on the riding part. After the game is done select one bigger kid to match with a smaller one and run through it once–both to illustrate your point and for your own enjoyment–because they will really move around that cone.

Activity #2: Dizzy Spoon Carry

This is another relay race.

Provide each team with a spoon and a rubber, bouncy ball–you decide how big each one should be. One by one each player will carry the ball on the spoon to the other end of the playing area. When they get to the cone they hand the spoon and ball to a leader, pick up the baseball bat, bend over it, placing their forehead on the end. They must then run around the bat, with the bat pointing down to the floor, five times–as fast as they can.

After five circles they drop the bat where it is and take the spoon and ball from the leader–who points them in the right direction. They must then return to their team and hand the spoon and ball to the next player–after crossing the line.

Provide one or two leaders in the center of the room to spot each dizzy kid and prevent collisions.

The first team finished, that is sitting quietly, wins the game.

Activity #3: Out of Control Nuke 'Em

Set up a room divider in the middle of the room to separate it into a two-sided court. The divider needs to be solid and taller than any of your players.

Proceed to play Nuke 'Em (volleyball but without hitting the ball—it can be caught and thrown over the divider—allow no more than two players to touch the ball before thrown over).

Add more balls once they get the hang of it. It will really get out of control—so will keeping score, but that's not all that important.

Activity #4: Out of Control Kickball

This is kickball with only one base, but many kickers each "up," and no requirement to leave the base and run home. Confused?

One team takes field while the other is kicking. The only base is the wall opposite the kicking end—the entire wall.

Place a line of masking tape on the floor a few feet out from the kicking team's wall. You could also put three small cross pieces of tape on the line to designate the spots to kick from but this is not absolutely necessary.

Place three balls on the kicking line—with a few feet in between them.

Up to three players can kick each time—but for each "Up" all kickers must kick at the same time. Once the ball is kicked the kicker must run to the other end of the playing area and touch the wall—or line if you can't use the wall. If they are touching the wall and have not gotten "out" they are safe until the next time they decide to run when a player(s) kicks. They do not have to run on a kick—they have the right to choose. If they do run, they must make it back to the other end of the playing area and cross the line without getting out in order to score a point. Once they leave the wall or line they are committed to running for a score—they cannot return to the base.

When a ball, or balls, is/are kicked the fielding team can use any of the kicked balls to get a runner out by getting it and throwing it at a running player and hitting them below the shoulders. If a runner is hit above the shoulders the runner is not out. If the ball is caught in the air the kicker is out. Runners on the wall do not have to tag up though.

Fielders Beware: Runners can dodge the balls (they cannot try to catch them though).

Each play ends when all the balls are returned to the line. Runners can still make a break for it if there is still a ball in play–even just one.

Don't count the outs for the inning–let every player kick. Obviously, safe runners can remain on the base as long as they want, but when the last kicker(s) is up it is also their last opportunity to run and score. The last kicker(s) only have that chance to score as well so look for some great action on that play.

Discussion: Jesus controls the storm and can control the storms in our lives if we let him.

Open with a clip from one of the following television shows or movies: Turner & Hooch, I Love Lucy–the candy factory episode or Cheaper By the Dozen (the 2003 version with Steve Martin). Turner & Hooch is recommended because the kids will love that the dog is out of control and the point is made with no dialogue. They are also not likely to have seen this movie before and won't know what is coming.

How would you like to have that dog sleep in your room (or reference the scene from the clip you chose to show)?

What would he do to your room?

He was pretty well out of control wasn't he? Do you think obedience school would help him or is he beyond hope?

There were some men in the Bible that felt, at one time, that there was no hope.

It was a day that Jesus had been teaching the entire day without a break. After He was done He and His disciples got into a boat and planned to go across a lake.

They got in the boat and Jesus decided to go and rest while they sailed. After a while a terrible storm came upon them. It may have felt like this to them...

\<Play clip from The Perfect Storm–the worst part of the storm, when the boat is in obvious peril–watch it ahead of time to make sure language is appropriate for your group of kids\>

How much hope do you have for that little boat in that terrible storm?

That's about as much hope as the disciples had on their boat in the terrible storm that came on them. They were terrified.

They ran to Jesus where He was sleeping and shouted, "Jesus! JESUS!! Don't you care if we drown?"

What do you think Jesus said?

He got up, very calmly–as if there were no storm at all. He said to His disciples, "Why are you so afraid?"

Okay–I have to admit that I would have been afraid myself. Wouldn't you?

He went on to say, "Have you no faith?"

Okay, again, I'd have to admit that I would have thought I was about to drown too. I probably would not have considered that there was a way to come out of that one alive. How would you have reacted to what Jesus said? (You could get some pretty fun answers here)

What happened next would have blown me away–just thinking about it blows me away now.

Jesus got up and went to the boat deck. The boat was tossing and turning. It would have been impossible to stand still on the boat, let alone walk to the bow. He raised His arms (imitate this) *and then scolded the wind and the waves. He stated firmly, "Quiet! Be Still!"*

And the wind and waves obeyed Him!! They went from completely out of control to calm and quiet.

Sometimes things are out of control in life. You may have a lot going on in your house–parents are busy, there is lots of activity, things to be done and never enough time to do them. It makes things seem crazy. When things are out of control the best way to find some peace and quiet is to go to Jesus and talk to Him. Things are never as out of control when you are talking to Him. The stuff may still be there to do and things may still be noisy and crazy, but you will find peace in Him.

Closing Activity: Out of Control Round Up

Have all kids create a circle but with their feet spread wide apart.

Select two or three players to be in the center. Provide each one with a supply of balls.

On "GO" the kids in the center begin rolling the balls as hard and fast as they can–trying to get the balls through the legs of everyone on the circle. Players on the circle defend their "goal" by bending at the waist and blocking the balls with their hands. They cannot squat down and they must spread feet wide enough to allow the ball through. They also are not allowed to put their hands and arms down in an attempt to block the goal completely and not have to move their arms–trust me they will try to do this.

Once a ball makes it through their legs they must stand up and put their hands behind their head–indicating they are out–but they remain on the circle.

The last one or two kids left bending on the circle win the round.

Everyone helps to collect the balls and returns them to the center buckets/baskets for the next round.

Select two or three new players for the rollers. Don't select based on winning or you will have a few kids that don't get to be in the center and a few that get multiple turns. Select based on who is yet to be in the center and in the order of good attitudes.

Alternate Activity: Out of Control Dodgeball (Change-Up Dodgeball)

This is likely to be everyone's favorite version of dodgeball once you play it.

In this version everyone is on his or her own team and can run anywhere. There is only one ball–preferably a really large ball, approximately 36." Bigens is a brand name for a large ball like this. It's a great addition to your supply closet too–for "Giant night," or to play this game as often as you need a filler activity for your kids.

How to play:

Just like regular dodgeball, you are out if you get hit with the ball directly. If it touches the ground first you are not out.

You are also out if you throw the ball at a player and they catch it. This is no easy task with this size ball—so it adds a degree of difficulty for the kids that normally get everyone out by catching a throw. They take more of a risk by trying to catch the ball.

The player that has the ball may only take one step with it–eliminating the dominant player that chases everyone down and gets him or her out. If they take more than one step with the ball they are out. There are ways to move with the ball that don't require holding on to it: Dribbling and rolling. The fun is that they are at risk of losing it since they must pick it up and throw it to get someone out. Steals are fun for the kids!!

When a player gets out they still need to pay attention to the game because when the players that got them out get out themselves they can return to the game—unlimited redemption! So the game is always changing and they don't have to wait for an ultimate winner to re-enter the game.

Players that get out by taking more than one step can re-enter if another kid gets out by doing the same thing or by allowance from the game leader. Don't make them sit out longer than normal, but do insist they sit out for breaking the rule.

By the way–this is a GREAT game for leaders to play too!!

Supplies Needed for "Out of Control" Based on Funds available			
Activity	Budget	Budget w/ some frills	Bells & Whistles
Crack the Whip	-Cones -2 Platform Scooters -2 jump ropes	Same	Same

Dizzy Spoon Carry	-Cones	Same	Same
	-2 big Spoons		
	-2 Rubber Balls		
	-2 Baseball Bats		
Out of Control Nuke 'Em	-Room Divider or curtain	Same	Same
	-Cones		
	-Masking tape		
	-Volleyball or kickball - several		
Discussion	-Bible	Same	Same
	-TV & VCR or DVD Player		
	-Turner & Hooch video or DVD – the scene where Turner leaves the dog alone, locked in a closet, and he breaks through the door and pretty well destroys the place. The kids will love this one!		
	-Or-		
	-I Love Lucy video or DVD – the episode where she is in the candy factory working the conveyer belt		
	-Or-		
	-Cheaper By The Dozen video or DVD – the scene at the breakfast table with the whole family trying to eat amongst the chaos		
	-Also, video or DVD of "The Perfect Storm" the scene at the worst of the storm when the waves are towering over the boat		
Out of Control Round Up	-Lots of safe balls that don't hurt if hit with them	Same	Same
	-Buckets or laundry baskets to collect balls		
Out of Control Dodgeball	-Giant Ball	Same	Same

Pressure

Theme Target:
Teach kids how to deal with pressure.

Golden Nugget:
Under Satan's pressure will you draw near to God or walk away?

Scripture:
Peter denying Christ. Mark 14:27–31; John 18:17; John 18:25–27; Mark 14:72 (The Message)

This is a great event, with a number of activities that you can play for quite a while. It could be used for a longer event–four hours or so, or remove some activities for a shorter time frame.

Activity # 1: Pressure Dodgeball (Extreme Dodgeball)

In this game the leaders get to have a ton of fun throwing balls at the kids. Give each leader a bucket and many balls that don't hurt in their bucket. Split the leaders so you have a few on both sides of the playing area–which should be a rectangle.

All the kids, no matter what team, should line up at one end of the playing area. Set up cones to designate the corners. On "GO" the kids must all run to the other end of the playing area. The leaders try to hit the kids by throwing the balls at them. Every player that makes it across the other end line stays in to go again. Any player that receives a direct hit before he crosses the line at the other end must sit down where he got hit. He now becomes an obstacle for the remaining kids to get past.

If your playing area is extremely large you could allow the ones that are sitting to be more than just obstacles–they could be taggers. While they must remain sitting and in their spot they could tag a player as he runs by and it be equivalent to a direct hit from a leader.

Play as many rounds as it takes to get down to one kid. The team that the last player represents receives points.

Play as long as you want or until the kids are growing tired of it–which will take a while.

Note: Be sure to use balls that don't hurt if a kid is hit in the face or head so you can avoid needing the rule that they must be hit from the neck down. Kids will cheat on this one if given an opening to do so.

Activity # 2: Sumo Tube

Make a square–approximately 12' x 12' to use as the playing area. Each team should be standing or sitting well outside of the playing square.

When you call a number the kid on each team that has that number comes to the center. You will give each one of them an inner tube and have them hold it around their waist. Once "tubed" up insist that they honor their opponent by bowing (You will have some kids that really play this up and bow like a sumo wrestler would–which is great fun).

Ask each one, individually, "Are you ready to rumble?" When you have received a "yes" from each one yell, "GO!"

On "go" they will each try to push the other one out of the playing area with their inner tube. They must keep both hands on the tube at all times so as not to push or hit with their hands. If a fall occurs pause the play and let the fallen player get up and reset.

The first player to step over the line of the playing box, if even just a toe, is the loser and both return to their team.

The kids will LOVE this game and, after all have gone, they will most likely ask if they can challenge a specific player. Allow this as you have time and as long as the other player accepts the challenge.

Activity # 3: Out of Control Round Up

Have all kids create a circle but with their feet spread wide apart.

Select two or three players to be in the center. Provide each one with a supply of balls.

On "GO" the kids in the center begin rolling the balls as hard and fast as they can—trying to get the balls through the legs of everyone on the circle. Players on the circle defend their "goal" by bending at the waist and blocking the balls with their hands. They cannot squat down and they must spread feet wide enough to allow the ball through. They also are not allowed to put their hands and arms down in an attempt to block the goal completely and not have to move their arms—trust me they will try to do this.

Once a ball makes it through their legs they must stand up and put their hands behind their head—indicating they are out—but they remain on the circle.

The last one or two kids left bending on the circle win the round.

Everyone helps to collect the balls and returns them to the center buckets/baskets for the next round.

Select two or three new players for the rollers. Don't select based on winning or you will have a few kids that don't get to be in the center and a few that get multiple turns. Select based on who is yet to be in the center and in the order of good attitudes.

Activity # 4: Criss Cross Crash

Create a large square or rectangular playing area by putting masking tape on the floor for lines if you don't already have lines on your floor.

Each team is divided in half. Each ½ team should be in a corner of the square/rectangle with opposing teams in adjoining corners–so that the leaders of both ½'s of each team are looking at each other across the diagonal like so:

1   2

☒

2   1

Provide a scooter to the first player in each corner.

On "GO" each player must get on their scooter and "scoot" across the diagonal to their team on the other corner and give the scooter to the next player in line once he clears the corner. This continues until all players on the team have crossed to the opposite corner.

Beware in the center: It can get really clogged in there! Sometimes the shortest distance isn't the best. You may have some kids that figure this out.

You can continue with additional rounds, with other ways of crossing. Some suggestions for crossing: hop on one foot; crawl; dribble a basketball or dribble a ball with a hockey stick.

Activity # 6: Pressure Cooker

One team stands in a circle surrounding a central thrower (the head).

The other team lines up outside the circle in a designated safe area–create a lane to the safe area.

It should look like this:

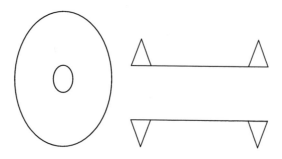

The player in the middle of the circle has to throw the ball to each of his/her team members in turn. He is responsible to keep track of how many catches were made.

Meanwhile, the members of the second team in turn have to run a relay around the circle. The next member waits and only takes off when the runner in front of him/her has returned through the lane, crosses the line and tags him.

When the last player in the running team has completed their circuit the timer stops. The running time is announced and the thrower of the first team says how many actual catches were made.

Teams then swap places. The running team tries to get all team members to complete the task in less time than the other team and the new circle tries to get more catches.

Play as many rounds as you want.

Discussion: How do you respond to Satan's Pressure?

Open with a demonstration:

We are going to talk about the affects of pressure today.

<Put a clean bottle on a table. >

Imagine this bottle is your direction in life–who you want to be, how you want to act, what you want to do.

<Pull out one hardboiled egg and put it on top of the bottle, little end down (with no matches inside).>

Now imagine that this is you–having to decide how to live your life. How do "you" get on with your life (how does the egg get into the bottle)? See what suggestions you get.

There is a lot of pressure placed on each one of us to live our lives a certain way, isn't there? Your parents tell you what to do. Your teachers tell you what to do. Your friends influence you.

A lot of times the pressure is good–it gently pushes us to reach our goals <gently push on the egg a little, trying to ease it into the bottle).

What happens when the pressure gets too great?

(Pound the egg with an open hand and jam it into the bottle–making sure the egg breaks up in the process)

Do you think that there is any way for you to live your life and be who you want to be without the pressure breaking you up?

Now do the experiment–set it up the same way but put the egg on with the big side down. When you light the matches compare the flame to the light of Jesus inside you.

When you accept Jesus into your life His love burns inside you. With Jesus in your life He draws you into Himself and you become the person He has planned for you to be.

Science Experiment: Egg in the Bottle

This is a really cool science experiment that will illustrate your point beautifully. You will need to try it ahead of time to see how it works and make sure you select the appropriate materials. If you are up to it—break up into groups, with one adult leader in each group, and allow the kids to do the experiment with only the directions as their guide, before you do it for everyone.

The experiment is very simple but you need to have the right size bottle. The bottle should have a long neck and the opening should be pretty wide–so the egg sits on top of the bottle comfortably without falling through—sixteen to twenty ounce iced tea bottles work well. Remove the label so you can see into the bottle easily.

Materials:

* ✶ Bottle–clean and completely dry, with label removed
* ✶ Hard-boiled egg–peeled–you could also use water balloons if you don't want to waste eggs
* ✶ Matches
* ✶ Strips of paper (if necessary)
* ✶ Copies of directions if you break up into groups

Here's what you do:

Light three matches and drop them into the bottle. They need to stay lit. If you are having trouble with this, light the strip of paper and put that into the bottle.

Quickly place the egg on top of the bottle–try it with the big end down first–that will keep the egg whole as it goes into the bottle. With the little end down the egg may break up as it is sucked into the bottle.

Watch as the egg gets sucked in–with a long necked bottle it will be pretty dramatic when it clears the neck! Be prepared to do this several times–it is really cool!

Supposedly you can get the egg back out of the bottle by holding the bottle above you and blowing into it when the egg reaches the neck. It may work if you put a straw into the bottle so it reaches past the egg when the egg comes down to the neck.

Once you have done this enough times to satisfy their enthusiasm— or you are out of materials—(which will probably happen first) continue the discussion.

That is exactly how pressure works on us. Pressure from the outside can be pretty powerful on us. It can weigh heavily and push too hard, sometimes forcing us to move in a direction we shouldn't go. When we allow that pressure to take over we end up hurt.

What kinds of pressure do you have on you?—You could get some pretty interesting answers on this one.

When we focus on God's love for us, and Christ's presence in our lives we are drawn into it. With Jesus as our guide we can get where we want to go and be the person He wants us to be, without breaking into pieces.

What about the pressure to be committed to Jesus? It can be hard sometimes to follow Jesus, especially when some people tell you it's not cool to be like Him. Don't worry… you are not the only one who has ever had a hard time being committed to Him when this happens. One of the guys that loved Him dearly, one of His own disciples, had a hard time with that same exact thing.

The last time Jesus was with his disciples–the guys that had been following Him while He was teaching and learning from Him - Jesus told them about the things that were soon going to happen… that He would be arrested and that would begin the journey to His death. Jesus knew

He had come to fulfill a plan, and that He had to die in order to do so. At this last supper with His friends He told them some things that didn't make sense to them. One of those things really bothered Peter.

Mark 14:27–31 (The Message)

> "You will all fall away," Jesus told them, "for it is written:" 'I will strike the shepherd, and the sheep will be scattered.' But after I have risen, I will go ahead of you into Galilee."
>
> Peter declared, "Even if all fall away, I will not."
>
> "I tell you the truth," Jesus answered, "today—yes, tonight—before the rooster crows twice you yourself will disown me three times."
>
> But Peter insisted emphatically, "Even if I have to die with you, I will never disown you." And all the others said the same.

Peter could not believe it. He loved Jesus and he would never act like he didn't know him.

Soon Jesus was arrested and things began to happen just like Jesus said they would. He was treated very badly by the people who were accusing Him of crimes. While all this was happening Jesus' friends were scared. People began questioning them to see if they had been following Jesus and had helped Him in His crimes.

Peter was waiting for Jesus as Jesus was being questioned. He was in a courtyard outside where Jesus was.

Mark 14:66–72 (The Message):

> While all this was going on, Peter was down in the courtyard. One of the Chief Priest's servant girls came in and, seeing Peter warming himself there, looked hard at him and said, "You were with the Nazarene, Jesus."
>
> He denied it: "I don't know what you're talking about." He went out on the porch. A rooster crowed.
>
> The girl spotted him and began telling the people standing around, "He's one of them." He denied it again.

After a little while, the bystanders brought it up again. "You've got to be one of them. You've got 'Galilean' written all over you."

Now Peter got really nervous and swore, "I never laid eyes on this man you're talking about." Just then the rooster crowed a second time. Peter remembered how Jesus had said, "Before a rooster crows twice, you'll deny me three times." He collapsed in tears.

Why did Peter say that He didn't know Jesus?

If it was difficult for Peter to stand up for Jesus, and He was a man who walked with Jesus and loved Him very much, then there will be times when it may be difficult for us too. It's not always the cool thing to follow Jesus. It's also not always the safe thing. But, just like in the science experiment, it is the thing that will get us to where God wants us to go!

I challenge you to stand up to the pressures that are on you to be someone you know God doesn't want you to be. Keep your focus on the fire of Jesus inside you and He will draw you closer to Him.

If you really want to explain the science behind the experiment here it is:

The flames heat the air in the bottle. As the heated air expands, some of it escapes out the bottle. When the matches go out, the air inside the bottle cools and contracts, thus creating a lower pressure inside the bottle than outside. The greater pressure outside the bottle forces the egg into the bottle.

Closing Activity: Pressure Dodgeball (a.k.a. Change-Up Dodgeball and Out of Control Dodgeball)

This is likely to be everyone's favorite version of dodgeball once you play it.

In this version everyone is on his or her own team and can run anywhere. There is only one ball–preferably a really large ball, approximately 36." Bigens is a brand name for a large ball like this. It's a great addition to your supply closet too–for "Giant night," or to play this game as often as you need a filler activity for your kids.

How to play:

Just like regular dodgeball, you are out if you get hit with the ball directly. If it touches the ground first you are not out.

You are also out if you throw the ball at a player and they catch it. This is no easy task with this size ball—so it adds a degree of difficulty for the kids that normally get everyone out by catching a throw. They take more of a risk by trying to catch the ball.

The player that has the ball may only take one step with it–eliminating the dominant player that chases everyone down and gets him or her out. If they take more than one step with the ball they are out. There are ways to move with the ball that don't require holding on to it: Dribbling and rolling. The fun is that they are at risk of losing it since they must pick it up and throw it to get someone out. Steals are fun for the kids!!

When a player gets out they still need to pay attention to the game because when the players that got them out get out themselves they can return to the game—unlimited redemption! So the game is always changing and they don't have to wait for an ultimate winner to re-enter the game.

Players that get out by taking more than one step can re-enter if another kid gets out by doing the same thing or by allowance from the game leader. Don't make them sit out longer than normal, but do insist they sit out for breaking the rule.

By the way–this is a *great* game for leaders to play too!!

Supplies Needed for "Pressure" Based on Funds available			
Activity	Budget	Budget w/ some frills	Bells & Whistles
Extreme Dodgeball	-Cones -1 bucket per leader -Lots of balls that don't hurt when hit in face (consider splash balls for extra fun)	Same	Same
Sumo Tube	-Masking tape -2 inner tubes – real or plastic inflatable pool rings	Same	Same

Out of Control Round Up	-Lots of safe balls that don't hurt if hit with them -Buckets or laundry baskets to collect balls	Same	Same
Criss Cross Crash	-Masking tape to make playing court -4 Platform Scooters -4 hockey sticks -4 small balls -4 bigger balls that bounce	Same	Same
Pressure Cooker	-1 Ball -4 cones -Stopwatch	Same	Same
Science Experiment	-Table -Clear, class bottles with long neck and 1 inch radius opening -Hard Boiled eggs – peeled -Matches -Strips of paper -Trash bag	Same but enough for you to do at least one demonstration and to break into groups and allow the kids to give it a try	Same but enough for you to do at least one demonstration and groups of 3 (1 adult and 2 kids) to give it a try
Discussion	-Bible		
Steal the Bacon – with tires or inner tubes	-Cones -Masking tape for lines -Tires or tubes -Whistle		

Salvation Invitation

The themes in this book are designed to provide opportunity to introduce kids to Christ. You could be working in a ministry that is focused on kids that don't know anything about God, the Bible or Jesus. If that is the case you are definitely in a position to show them the Way to be saved.

You also may be working with kids that have grown up in the church and have been offered the invitation to accept Christ many times before. That doesn't mean they have accepted it though.

Unless you know, without a doubt, that each child in front of you has accepted Christ as their savior you should assume that you need to be prepared to offer the invitation to them to do so when you see an opportunity before you.

In order to offer an invitation when the opportunity is there you need to be comfortable with the aspects of it. It can be overwhelming to be the person called to detail the specifics, knowing that you are influencing the most important and amazing decision they will ever make, but it is very simple and kids can easily understand it. You must not be nervous about it–it needs to feel like these are the most natural words you can speak.

Here are the points that need to be covered:

- ★ Every person is a sinner. It is how we are born. The Bible tells us that there is not a single person that has ever lived, except for Jesus, who did not sin. (Romans 3:23)

- ★ The Bible also tells us that the punishment for sin is death–not our bodies, but the soul of who we are. (Romans 6:29)

- ★ God loves each of us very, very much–more than any person ever could. (John 3:16)

- ★ Because He loves us He gave us the way to pay for our sins. (John 3:16) He gave us Jesus, to act for us by dying on the cross. Jesus was the only choice because He was God's perfect Son and that made Him the perfect sacrifice to die in our place.

- ★ After Jesus died for us He rose from the dead to prove that He was able to defeat death. (Luke 24)

- ★ Jesus has gone to prepare a place in Heaven (John 14:2) for everyone that believes that He is the way, the truth and the life (John 14:6) and will come again for them.

Writing the invitation out in your own words will make you more comfortable with it. For a starting place you could work with something like this:

Right now I want to give you the opportunity to make the most important decision you will ever make. God loves you and sent His Son, Jesus, for you. Jesus wants nothing more than to be a part of your life, but it is up to you to choose Him. Nobody can choose Him for you. He is waiting for you to invite Him into your life.

It is very simple and only requires you to talk to Him. You don't have to talk out loud–He will hear you, but you do need to tell Him a few things.

If you have never asked Jesus to come into your life and you want to do that right now I will tell you how. Close your eyes so you can focus on what you need to do and what you are saying to Him.

First, you need to tell Him that you know that you are a sinner because everyone is a sinner and you are no different than anyone else.

Second, you need to tell Him that you understand that the punishment for being a sinner is death and hell for those who die.

Third, you believe that God loves you and sent Jesus to take your punishment because you couldn't pay for your sins yourself.

Fourth, you believe that He died for you and then rose again to beat death.

Finally, ask Him to come into your heart and life and to be with you always as your Lord.

And just like that you have asked Him to come into your heart and He did. From this moment on you will never be without Him.

It is important, after you finish the prayer, that you ask that if anyone just made that decision for the first time in their life that they raise their hand for you to see it. If anyone raises his or her hand you need to celebrate. Congratulate them and tell them that at that very moment there is a party in Heaven, in their honor, and the angels are rejoicing because of the new place in Heaven reserved for them.

It really is cause for celebration and you should personally welcome them into the Family of God. You should also follow it up with a note or card, or even a small, meaningful poster that acknowledges their acceptance of Christ. A personal note written on the back of it, with the date of their new birthday is an added touch that will mean more to them than you may ever know.